D0897813

THE ROAD TO ETERNAL LIFE

The Road to Eternal Life

Reflections on
the Prologue of Benedict's Rule

Michael Casey, OCSO

LITURGICAL PRESS
Collegeville, Minnesota

www.litpress.org

Imprimi potest. Abbot David G. Tomlins, OCSO
7 December 2010

1   2   3   4   5   6   7   8

Library of Congress Cataloging-in-Publication Data

Casey, Michael, 1942–
    The road to eternal life : reflections on the Prologue of
Benedict's Rule / Michael Casey.
        p.   cm.
    ISBN 978-0-8146-3384-7 — ISBN 978-0-8146-3954-2 (e-book)
    1. Benedict, Saint, Abbot of Monte Cassino. Regula. Prologus.
2. Benedictines—Spiritual life.   3. Meditations.   I. Title.

BX3004.Z5C338 2011
255'.106—dc22   2011016486

Contents

Preface

These reflections began life as a yearlong series of ten-minute talks made available each week during 2010 on the Tarrawarra Abbey website. Each talk took as its starting point a verse of the Prologue of the Rule of Saint Benedict and mulled over it, drawing on other passages from the Rule, themes from monastic tradition, and my own life experience to try to come to appreciate what Saint Benedict was saying.

To the best of my knowledge, this is the first time the Prologue has been submitted to such intensive comment. There are many books available dealing with "Benedictine spirituality," but not many of these submit themselves to the discipline of sustained attention to the text of the Rule. I have chosen to do a close reading of Saint Benedict's text in the hope that less of what he intended to say will escape me. This involves paying close attention to every word and every phrase. To help me in this I have retranslated the text, not because existing translations are inadequate, but because it compelled me to gauge carefully the exact meaning of every verse.

Strictly speaking, these talks are not a commentary. I have termed them simply "reflections." They are closest to the writings of the twelfth-century Cistercians, like Bernard of Clairvaux, who have influenced me so greatly. These were termed *sermones*, not "sermons" as we know them, but familiar talks, using the text as a springboard or point of departure. The content of these talks was not always predictable, although they circled around a few strong themes and were always focused firmly on practical Christian living in daily life. They were meant to help the listeners to build a bridge between the text and their own lives and, thus, to invite them to keep drawing from their own meditations the inspiration for a better life.

I have chosen as my base text the Prologue of Saint Benedict's Rule. Although the bulk of this long preliminary section is drawn from his principal source, the so-called Rule of the Master, it remains a fair indication of the background to Saint Benedict's thinking that is evident in the more practical portions of the Rule. It is the backdrop against which takes place all the drama of monastic life. Alas, sometimes we get so caught up in the details that we fail to watch the tides but, instead, concentrate on the eddies.

The alert reader will notice my indebtedness to the work of the masterful commentators with which our generation is blessed. I note, in particular, that I have profited much from the work of Aquinata Böckmann, Terrence Kardong, Michaela Puzicha, and Adalbert de Vogüé, though I can scarcely hold them responsible for any errors I have made.

There is much repetition in the Prologue, which invites the lazy commentator to take a shortcut by combining two or three verses together. I have resisted this temptation on the ground that if Saint Benedict considered a theme important enough to bear repeating, then the commentator should follow his example. The fact that the reflections were composed on a stop-and-go basis, with about a week between their composition, meant that after a lapse in time my take on a particular theme was often slightly different. If I were to repeat the exercise in five years' time, the end product would most likely be significantly different.

These reflections are probably best read in the manner that they were written: one at a time, spread out, maybe, over the course of a year. Their purpose is not to deliver a neatly packaged and definitive set of considerations for each verse but to invite readers to continue the process for themselves, aligning the text with their own experience and allowing it to speak to their lives.

As many have noted, the opening word of the Rule is "Listen!" I have tried to listen to what the text was saying as I wrote and also to listen to my own life. I hope readers will do the same. In this manner the Rule will have a formative influence on their life and spirituality, providing a complement to contemporary sources of guidance. But, first, all of us, you and I, must learn to listen and so to become genuine disciples in the school of the Lord's service.

I have given this series of talks the title *The Road to Eternal Life* because I have come to the conclusion that this is really Saint Benedict's principal concern in the Prologue: to map out for us the road that leads to heaven. Behind this image is the theme of the journey. This metaphor refers not so much to the glamorous luxury of airline advertisements but to the hard and rough going that was typical of travel in the ancient world, with few conveniences and many dangers. The journey is tolerable only because of a lively hope of arriving at the desired destination; to lose sight of the goal renders the traveling meaningless.

The Rule was written for monks and when I am speaking of Saint Benedict's own context I usually frame my remarks in a male and monastic context. As often as possible in the rest of these reflections, I have tried to twist the syntax to ensure that neither women disciples of Saint Benedict nor those who do not live in monasteries may feel excluded. I ask readers' indulgence if I have not been perfectly successful in this endeavor.

The translations of all biblical and patristic texts are my own. I have followed the Vulgate numbering of the Psalms, as used by Saint Benedict; usually it is one less than the Hebrew numbering found in most modern versions. For the rest, sit back and enjoy the flight.

Saint Benedict's Rule for Monasteries

The Prologue

[1]Son, listen to the instructions of a master. Bend the ear of your heart to receive gladly the advice of a kind father, and fulfill it in practice. [2]In this way, by the labor of obedience, you will return to him from whom you have withdrawn by the slackness of disobedience.

[3]Now my discourse is directed to you, whoever you are, who renounce the movements of self-will and, being ready to fight for the Lord Christ, the true King, take up the strong and distinguished weapons of obedience. [4]First, whenever you begin to do some good deed, ask [Christ] with most insistent prayer that he bring it to completion. [5]In this way, [Christ] who has been pleased to count us in the number of his sons will not ever be grieved by our evil deeds.

[6]Thus we must obey him at all times through his good things in us, so that he will not, in time, disinherit us as an angry father [disinherits] his sons. [7]Also he will not, as a fearsome Lord, angry because of our evil deeds, hand us over to perpetual punishment like the most wicked of slaves who were not willing to follow him to glory.

[8]Now, therefore, let us finally arise. Scripture stirs us up saying, "Now is the hour to rise from sleep." [9]And with eyes wide open to the divinizing light, and with astonished ears, let

us hear God's voice crying out to us every day and admonishing us. [10]"Today, if you hear [God's] voice, harden not your hearts." [11]And again, "Let the one who has ears for hearing, hear what the Spirit says to the churches." [12]And what does [the Spirit] say? "Come, children, listen to me; I will teach you fear of the Lord." [13]"Run while you have the light of life, lest the darkness of death envelop you."

[14]And the Lord, seeking his workman in the midst of a multitude of people, cries out to him and says: [15]"Who is the person who wants life and desires to see good days?" [16]If hearing this, you respond, "I do," the Lord says this to you. [17]"If you want to have true and perpetual life, forbid your tongue from evil and your lips lest they speak deceit. Turn away from evil and do good. Seek peace and pursue it." [18]"And when you have done this, my eyes will be upon you and my ears [will be attentive] to your prayers. Before you call upon me I shall say to you, 'Here I am.'" [19]What is sweeter for us, dearest brothers, than this voice of the Lord inviting us? [20]Behold, in his kindness the Lord is showing us the road of life.

[21]Therefore, with our loins girded with faith and the observance of good deeds, let us set out on his journeys with the guidance of the Gospel, so that we may be worthy to see the one who has called us into his kingdom. [22]We cannot arrive at the tent of this kingdom in which we want to dwell, except by running there by means of good deeds.

[23]Let us, however, ask the Lord with the prophet, and say to him: "Lord who will dwell in your tent? Who will find rest on your holy mountain?" [24]After this question, brothers, let us listen to the Lord answering, showing us the road to his tent. [25]He says: "The one who enters without stain and practices righteousness." [26]"The one who speaks truth in the heart and does not commit deceit with the tongue." [27]"The one who does no evil to a neighbor or allows dishonor against a neighbor." [28]"One who rejects and annihilates the malign devil when he suggests something, [driving him] out of sight

of the heart; one who grabs the thoughts born of him and beats them against [the rock that is] Christ."

29Those who fear the Lord are not elated by their good observance, but consider that the good things in them cannot have come about from themselves but are from the Lord. 30And so they magnify the Lord working in them, saying with the prophet: "Not to us, Lord, not to us, but to your name give the glory." 31In the same way, Paul the Apostle did not attribute anything of his preaching to himself but said, "It is by God's grace that I am what I am." 32And again he says, "Let the one who boasts, boast in the Lord."

33Whence the Lord says in the Gospel, "The one who hears these my words and does them, I will liken to a wise man who built his house on rock. 34The floods came, the winds blew and assailed that house and it did not fall, because its foundations were on rock."

35Having finished this, the Lord waits for us every day to respond by deeds to his holy admonitions. 36Because of this he has declared a truce during the days of this life to give us the opportunity to amend evils. 37As the Apostle says, "Do you not know that the patience of God is leading you on to repentance?" 38For the kind Lord says, "I do not want the death of sinners but that they may be converted and live."

39Brothers, since we have asked the Lord about those who dwell in his tent, and we have heard the instructions for dwelling [in that place] we have to do the duty of one who dwells there. 40Therefore our hearts and bodies must be prepared to serve under the instructions of holy obedience. 41For what is less possible for us by nature, let us ask the Lord that he may provide it for us by the help of his grace. 42And if we flee the punishments of hell, because we wish to arrive at unending life, 43then, while there is opportunity and we are in this body, and there is opportunity to complete [these tasks] by this light of life, 44there is a need to run and do now what will profit us in perpetuity.

⁴⁵Therefore a school of the Lord's service is to be set up by us. ⁴⁶In its organization we hope to put in place nothing that is harsh or heavy. ⁴⁷It may be a little restrictive—as reason and equity dictate—for the purpose of advancing the process of amending vices and for maintaining charity. ⁴⁸Do not run away from this road to salvation, fearful and terrified. At the very beginning it cannot be other than narrow. ⁴⁹As progress is made in the way of life and in faith, the road of God's commandments will be run with heart enlarged and in the indescribable sweetness of love. ⁵⁰And so, let us never cease to have [Christ] as master, let us persevere in his doctrine in the monastery until death, and let us participate by patience in the sufferings of Christ. In this way will we deserve to be sharers in his kingdom. Amen.

Introduction

The Purpose of the Prologue

The Rule of Saint Benedict is a rule—this is something that we must never forget. It is concerned principally to outline the rudiments of a monastic way of life that is conducive to living in substantial fidelity to the Gospel. If you look through the Rule's table of contents you can verify this for yourself. Benedict talks about food and drink and clothing, about what the monks do at different times of the day and in different seasons, how the liturgy is to be arranged, and the choreography of meals. He gives us rules for governance and procedures for admitting newcomers to the community. There can be no doubt that this is a pragmatic document, designed to create an oasis of order and discipline in a century when Italian society was torn apart by serial wars and their consequences. This is a how-to book—how to organize a community of men so that they can realistically undertake the long journey of seeking and finding God.

For many modern readers who approach the Rule hoping to find inspiration for their own journey, first contact can be disappointing. There seems to be an unbridgeable gap between that situation that Saint Benedict envisages and the world in which they live; his concerns do not reflect their own. Many of our contemporaries wonder how the Rule of Saint Benedict could have lasted so long when so much of its contents is out of date. So many measures are antiquated and quaint that they may be amusing to read but are scarcely likely to be put into practice.

This is so. The value of Benedict's Rule for the modern reader is less in his practical institutions than in the way these prescriptions embody beliefs and values that transcend the particular expressions that Benedict considered appropriate. Sometimes these beliefs and values are stated explicitly; at other times they have to be sought with more assiduity. It has to be admitted that the message of the Rule does not yield itself to cursory perusal. It will give itself up only to a close and intelligent reading of the text in which every word is weighed and the meaning of every sentence pondered.

The fact of the matter is that much of the Rule is not original. Benedict's concern was not to write something new but to compile a handbook that would embody the best of what ancient monastic tradition had to offer. He says as much in the final chapter, telling us to check out his sources if we want more detailed background to his prescriptions. Critical study of the Rule, much aided by technology, has uncovered most of these sources so that it becomes possible to see Benedict's hand at work in selecting what he will transmit, in omitting what he considers less valuable, in modifying the material he uses and adding to it, and, most interesting of all, in writing something that is completely his own.

Benedict's principal source is a long Italian rule written in the early 500s and usually given the title the Rule of the Master. This is rather an eccentric document and it is extremely doubtful that it was ever put into practice in real life. The Rule of the Master is an impractical and even occasionally bizarre text that Benedict needed to edit severely to ensure that only the wholesome elements of the Master's message were preserved. It does have the merit of providing a detailed description of an ideal form of monastic life that is in continuity with the classical monastic sources and somewhat adapted to the changing times. Benedict took over the basic structure, copied and adapted some of his observances, and recycled those passages in which the Master transmits fundamental monastic doctrine.

This process of adaptive borrowing is very clear in the Prologue. Of Benedict's text, forty verses out of fifty are directly from the Rule of the Master, reproducing that document's commentary on Psalms 14 and 33. More than two-thirds of the Master's text, including his commentary on the Lord's Prayer, has been omitted. It can be taken for granted that Benedict, although for the most part he is using another man's words, is expressing sentiments that are his own. The warm, interpersonal tone that is markedly present in the Prologue is to be assumed to be expressive of Benedict's attitude throughout the Rule, even though the matter with which he is dealing does not offer much scope for its direct expression.

There are some important themes that come to the surface in the Prologue. Of these we will speak in a general way in the next section.

Some Themes in the Prologue

It does not take a great deal of research to catch on to the preeminent theme of Saint Benedict's Prologue; it is a call to action. Listen to this roll call of verbs directed to the reader: "Listen . . . fulfill . . . labor . . . fight . . . rise up . . . run . . . do good . . . seek . . . pursue . . . set out . . . respond by deeds . . . amend evils." It is clear that Saint Benedict does not view the monastery as a pious country club in which the monks lounge around all day waiting to be sanctified. Those who enter a monastery are turning their backs on an easygoing life and committing themselves to positive effort to make possible their dreams of spiritual advancement. Monastic life is like active service in the army; it is like competing in high-level athletic contests. More realistically, monastic life is like the humdrum daily activity of laboring in a workshop, making use of a variety of implements to produce different results. This is the image that Saint Benedict develops at length in chapter 4, where he lists no fewer than seventy-four implements that the monk must employ, as circumstances warrant.

In the ancient way of looking at spiritual progress, the "active life" was seen as the beginning and foundation of all that followed. What was meant by this term "active life" was a phase in which the beginner monk took positive steps to acquire the virtues that would stand him in good stead in the years to follow. Of course, acquiring virtues seems like a worthwhile project, but its dynamics confuse many. Experience confirms that there are two preliminary phases to pass through before it becomes possible to make much progress in acquiring virtues. The first is self-knowledge—to become aware of our unconscious resistance to the call of God, which expresses itself both at the level of thought and in actions. The second is struggling against these embedded tendencies, failing often, and learning thereby to rely more on the help of God's grace than on our own desires for self-improvement. Virtues do not grow in a vacuum; they develop only in the context of struggling against our own particular vices. So the perspective in which the whole Rule needs to be read is that it provides for the beginnings of good monastic living (RB 73.1) by taking care, first of all, to neutralize vices so that, then, it becomes possible to nurture the growth of love (RB Prol. 47). This dynamic is very clearly detailed in Benedict's seventh chapter, which describes progress in terms of the ladder of humility.

This emphasis on living a good life by turning away from evil and being proactive in doing good has its own dangers. Principal among them is the possibility that we leave God out of the equation and try to go it alone. When this happens all progress is stymied. Instead of being a call coming from outside ourselves to go beyond our limits, the attraction to a spiritual life becomes instead an instrument of self-will. We fall into the tyranny of the superego, which enslaves instead of liberates. We are constantly aiming at a perfection that we ourselves have imagined without any reference to God's plans for us or, indeed, without any recognition of who we truly are and what our final goal might be.

Fortunately this iron will for self-improvement is ineffective and so we constantly fall short of the dubious ideals we had set up for ourselves. At this point we are confronted by two negative possibilities and one positive possibility. The negative possibilities are these: first, we make up our minds to try harder, surrounding ourselves with self-made rules that are not life-giving; second, we lose heart and abandon our spiritual aspirations, writing off our losses as experience gained, and try to live with reduced ideals. The positive possibility resulting from our failure and chronic recidivism is that we turn to God with a strong sense of urgency, recognizing that the only thing we can make of our lives is a mess and calling out to be saved. We trust no longer in our own power of accomplishment but only in God's grace.

Not surprisingly, alongside Benedict's emphasis on the active life, we find a complementary emphasis on reliance on grace. Every good action is to be accompanied by prayer; it is the inspired Scripture that rouses us from sleep; it is the divine light that opens our eyes, just as it is the divine voice that sharpens our sense of hearing. Our work is a response to God's daily call to conversion, calling us back from being lost and showing us the path that leads to everlasting life. The way will be long and toilsome, but it will be the Lord who helps us traverse it. There will be no scope for elation because it will be the Lord who accomplishes in us the good works of which we ourselves are incapable. "For what is less possible for us by nature, let us ask the Lord that he may provide it for us by the help of his grace."

There is a reason for this emphasis on the role of grace. The Rule of Saint Benedict was written at a time when various forms of what has been called "Pelagianism" were rampant in the church. Whether it ever actually existed is a moot point, but those who were passionate about the primacy of divine grace had a lot of fun contrasting their positions with this presumed heresy. Nevertheless, there was a tendency in monastic circles to speak so much about the moral implications of Christian faith that its divine and sacramental dimensions seem to have been left aside. Even John Cassian, one of Benedict's principal sources, was not exempt from charges that he was guilty of this. Benedict is protecting himself and rounding out his teaching on the active life by giving appropriate emphasis to the fact that it is God who begins the process of sanctification, it is God who sustains it day by day, and it is God who will bring it to completion.

It is in this context that we can better understand Benedict's insistence on obedience. For Benedict this is more than external compliance with external norms or external commands. In the first place it is heartfelt submission to God—our Creator, Sustainer, and the one who leads us to a life that is abundant beyond our power to conceive. This submission is not passivity. Obedience is, as Benedict insists, a labor; its opposite is inactivity, slackness, unconcern, procrastination. The purpose of obedience is to deliver us from the crippling deference we give to the impulses of self-will that enclose us in our own little world and block us from emerging into the full freedom to which we have been called. Later Benedict will stigmatize self-will as a false obedience: obeying our own desires and pleasures (RB 5.12). Acts of obedience to the Rule, to regulations, and to those who hold Christ's authority are merely external expressions of this more fundamental submission. Divorced from a lively attachment to God's will and the desire to adhere to it, this external compliance is no more than institutional subservience; it is not life-giving.

One element of the Prologue that may surprise modern readers is the insistence with which Benedict locates the choice of a good life as the choice between heaven and hell. We may find the language unappealing, but what he is trying to do is to show us that there is an eternal significance in every small choice that we make. Whenever we are confronted with a decision about what to do, Benedict wants us to see it not as a trivial exercise but as something of eternal significance. Each choice that we make reflects the goal we have embraced in our life. Do we choose life through our adherence to God's will? Or are we still bemired in the morass of self-will? As he will later write, "There are paths which seem humanly right whose end plunges into the depths of hell" (RB 7.21). Life, in all its ordinariness, is a drama in which every thought, word, and deed have serious consequences. This is a theme that will be more fully explored in the first step of the ladder of humility.

Benedict brings all these themes together in his presentation of the monastery as a school of the Lord's service. Here we are able to learn what we have not hitherto learned; here we are able to relearn what we have mislearned in the past. The task of scaling the Lord's high mountain is very great; it is beyond our capabilities. But Benedict is proposing to teach us how to do what we have to do, and how to allow God to do what God has to do. He is not severe in imparting his doctrine, though he is insistent; he does not consider it kindness to allow us to go astray and be lost. He is moderate in his demands, but they are demands; Benedict knows from experience that a life without discipline quickly becomes directionless. Monastic life, spiritual life, is all about becoming a learner, a disciple. It is not just a matter of doing but a matter of first learning and then doing.

And whose disciple are we to become? There is no question about this. We are to become ever more fully Christ's disciples. Benedict sees himself as a teacher in Christ's school; it is Christ's doctrine that he aims to impart. And how do we become disciples of Christ? Fundamentally, by taking the Gospel as our guide, allowing ourselves to be formed by the example of Jesus and by his teaching, so that by living as he lived and sharing his sufferings we may be found worthy to become with him the coheirs of the kingdom of heaven.

Son, listen to the instructions of a master. Bend the ear of your heart to receive gladly the advice of a kind father, and fulfill it in practice.

The paths to be taken in the spiritual journey are not self-evident. Although the desire and the energy to engage in the search for God may arise unbidden from within, it is not always clear how such energies may be channeled so that their purpose may be realized effectively. Without a spiritual guide, it is easy to squander these precious gifts in pursuits that lead nowhere. After a time, discouragement sets in that causes the journey to be abandoned.

The first step to be taken is to accept that if we aspire to travel to regions beyond our personal experience, we need the help of a mentor who has already made some progress in the journey we wish to undertake, a person who has the skills to explain to us how to proceed. We need to become disciples of a master. The ordinary consequence of committing ourselves seriously to the spiritual life is the willingness to submit our lives to the judgment and guidance of another.

There is a question here of something deeper than external submission. By exhorting us to "bend the ear of the heart," Saint Benedict is indicating that, in the act of listening to outward guidance, we also hear the internal echo of the words spoken. One of the signs of good spiritual masters is that they are able to express in words what we are feeling in the depths of our being. They give us a vocabulary to describe what we are experiencing. Rather than merely issuing prescriptions about what we are to do, a good mentor helps us to understand who we are and what we are. It is from this deeper self-understanding that clarity comes about practical choices.

Having said this, it is clear that we do not all have the good fortune to find such an outstanding spiritual guide. The next best option is to attach ourselves to a tradition, making the journey in company with others who share the same ideals and learning from their example and wisdom. If we cannot find a spiritual home in a community, then perhaps we need to seek guidance through disciplined reading.

In all these means of direction, discernment is necessary. An ordinary test that we can apply is to determine whether the guidance we are receiving is twofold—if it is a source of both comfort and challenge. If a person, group, or book only affirms and encourages us without ever challenging and calling us to conversion, then it is unlikely to be life-giving on a long-term basis. The same is true, though less usual, if our source of guidance challenges us without consoling us, in such a situation we will probably turn aside before very long.

Our opportunities will vary according to our particular situation and may change in the course of a lifetime. The important principle is, however, that we do seek to be guided on our way to God, believing that if we are sincere in our search God will never leave us without indications of the way that leads to life.

In this way, by the labor of obedience, you will return to him from whom you have withdrawn by the slackness of disobedience.

The ultimate goal of monastic life and of all spiritual endeavor is union with Christ. Saint Benedict sees movement in this direction as a "return," in the manner of the prodigal son—a return to the innocence with which we were graced at the time of our baptism and thereby a return to a loving intimacy with God our Father.

To return involves a change in direction, a conversion, which is at first interior but which must progressively make its way outward to mold both individual actions and habitual behavior. Seeking God requires conversion of heart and amendment of life. There is no other way.

Once we have turned around we need to move forward, slowly at first but with greater speed as progress ensues. This movement may be characterized as a movement from absence to presence—from a life in which Christ seemed to be absent toward a life in which every avenue to Christ's presence is explored. In particular this is a journey from forgetfulness of God to mindfulness, a theme that Saint Benedict will discuss in his treatment of the first step of the ladder of humility in chapter 7 of his Rule.

The "labor of obedience" is the means by which the goal of union with God is reached. Saint Benedict will later warn the newcomer that the way to God passes through harsh and rugged country; no one will complete this journey who is not robust and resilient and who is not prepared to work hard and to deal with reversals of every kind.

You will notice that the contrast that Saint Benedict makes is not between "submission" and "rebellion" or between "dependence" and "autonomy" but between "labor" and "slackness." What is being suggested here is that the major obstacle to spiritual growth is inactivity, taking things easy, letting things look after themselves. Like the lost souls in Saint Matthew's judgment scene, we will be amazed to find that it has been our sins of omission that have caused us the most damage. A *laissez-faire* attitude that avoids exertion or any expenditure of effort is the most likely cause of any retardation of spiritual growth. Active malevolence is much rarer than we may imagine; we sin most often by not caring enough to do the good that lies within our power.

It is fairly obvious that we need a spurt of energy to get us started on the spiritual pursuit; it is less obvious that the "labor of obedience" continues throughout life; we can never afford to relax our efforts and coast. Even when years of faithful practice have allowed for the development of habits of virtue so that good living becomes something like second nature to us, we need to remain both vigilant and energetic. In fact, the more virtuous we become the more demanding our conscience is, so that often we are asked to expend more effort in remaining faithful the further we have traveled along the road.

It is clear that, for Saint Benedict, faith needs to be supplemented by grace-inspired good works. You only have to look at his extensive list of "implements of good works" in chapter 4. It is our enthusiasm for the "labor of obedience" that signals the reality of our faith. Our time on earth is a period for working; it is only in eternity that we will be able to take our rest.

Now my discourse is directed to you, whoever you are, who renounce the movements of self-will and, being ready to fight for the Lord Christ, the true King, take up the strong and distinguished weapons of obedience.

Saint Benedict addresses the reader using the second-person pronoun in the singular, emphasizing that he is speaking in a personal way to each individual reader. It is, as was said in the opening verse, "the advice of a kind father" that each is to take to heart. In this way the Prologue takes the material prescriptions that follow in the body of the Rule out of the sphere of law and reframes them in the context of wisdom. The only authority that Benedict claims is the moral authority of long experience—not only his own, but also the age-old monastic tradition to which he gives voice.

What advice does this kind father have for one starting out on a spiritual journey? It is twofold. We are to renounce self-will, and we are to see our spiritual adventure less in terms of a personal project than as enrolling in the army of Christ our true King. And he wants the disciple to be ready for the struggle.

Why does Saint Benedict place so much emphasis on the renunciation of self-will? What does he mean by it? It is clear from the examination of the Rule as a whole that when Benedict speaks about self-will he is not referring to mature adult choices made in full freedom. He is thinking of something else entirely—those movements from deep inside us that are the source of all selfish behavior, self-centeredness, and self-promotion. We may ask, "What is wrong with such tendencies?"

The first thing that is wrong with them is that they influence our behavior in a way that short-circuits the operation of the mind and the will. We do not know where these impulses come from; we are conscious of their urgency and strength but we are not fully aware of why they are pushing us in a particular direction and why the last thing that they want us to do is to slow down and take our time to examine their suggestions rationally. If we allow ourselves to be propelled into action by the movements of self-will, we will find ourselves wondering afterward why we did what we did and unable to provide any rational explanation. Self-will bypasses the reason and leads us to consent unthinkingly to courses of action that are unhealthy in the long term. A drunk who drives does not consider the disastrous consequences of such an action and cannot be convinced of its danger. When we act under the influence of self-will the same happens. We go forward blindly, perhaps relishing the pleasures of the moment, unable to take into consideration its long-term effects.

The best indication that self-will is at work is to see what happens when its suggestions are blocked. A common result is rage or tantrum behavior, which is an infantile way of creating a storm in order to avoid a rational and adult interaction with reality. Who can argue with a hurricane? The last thing that self-will wants is to have its suggestions examined in the light of reason, by reference to ultimate principles, or in their consistency with personal integrity. Self-will is a tyrant, ruling below the threshold of consciousness; it demands an obedience that is immediate and absolute.

Benedict's way of escaping self-will, as he clearly indicates in chapter 5, is to live a communal life, accepting its structures and deferring to its legitimate authority. This makes possible an examined life—a life in which all the promptings that rise from the unconscious can be tested in the context of external reality. Obedience, we must insist, is not simply a means of social control; it is fundamentally an ascetical path to freedom from the tyranny of self-will and the means of living an adult life of integrity and consistency, one that conducts us toward the goal we have chosen. Without such freedom no progress in the contemplative life is possible. Saint Benedict will have much more to say about this topic. Obedience for him is not a servile escape from adult responsibility but, rather, the effective and distinguished means of achieving what we had set out to do—to turn away from evil and come close to God.

We do not do this alone, nor even only in the company of like-minded comrades. Our service is an act of loyalty to Christ. It is in his army that we fulfill our military obligations. He is our captain. We are guided by his principles and we follow his strategy. And so it is with the guidance of the Gospel that our campaign begins, continues, and arrives at completion. The monk freely chooses to follow Christ, not the impulses and tendencies of self-will. It is this personal linkage with Christ that will sustain him whatever hard and difficult things may come his way.

4

First, whenever you begin to do some good deed, ask [Christ] with most insistent prayer that he bring it to completion.

What a wonderful world it would be if we all kept our New Year's resolutions! If every time we started something worthwhile we stayed with it until it was complete! The sad reality is, however, that even our best inspirations often go unfulfilled simply because we do not persevere in their pursuit.

This is often the case in the spiritual life: people who have been experiencing a profound dissatisfaction with the level of fulfillment that material and temporal activities provide may suddenly get a glimpse into the reality of the spiritual world and are strongly attracted by it. They resolve to turn over a new leaf, to change their lives, to give more time for God and for prayer in their lives. And so they do. But it doesn't last long. Real and imagined urgencies rise up to swallow the time they had allocated for their interior life. A day goes by; next time a week goes by, and, before they know it, the program of spiritual practice that they had embraced has been left aside. What was well begun never came to completion.

Saint Benedict places much emphasis on stability and perseverance throughout his Rule. Without endurance and continuance, virtue has no lasting impact. He seems conscious that many good inspirations are begun but not finished, and so, even as we begin to rededicate our time to the service of Christ, he would have us be aware that it is unlikely to bear permanent fruit if we rely on our own efforts. He recommends that, even at its inception, every worthwhile initiative be accompanied by prayer, that it be done in the context of Christ, that we be mindful of its spiritual significance even as we begin it.

What does it mean to begin every good deed with sincere prayer? It is to acknowledge, first of all, that every good inspiration has its origins in the actions of God deep within us. We are being called to share in God's work by our simple acts of kindness, by our fidelity, by our generosity with our gifts and our time. Since these benevolent actions often go unrecognized and unrewarded in this life, we may easily tire of doing good and prefer to wait for others to do good for us. We lose heart and the will to continue weakens. To be "tireless in doing good" takes much courage—and this virtue comes only through sustained contact with Christ in prayer. Without prayer we quickly become discouraged.

To begin a good deed with prayer means to recognize that the inspiration to do good comes from God. It is to affirm our own need to be sustained by grace if we are to continue in doing good. It is the realistic acknowledgment that our contribution can go only so far; for our activity to be truly life-giving the intervention of God's redemptive grace is an absolute necessity. An act of kindness may be misread, a word of wisdom misunderstood, trust given abused, a good deed distorted by a wrong intention—unless the grace of God surrounds both giver and receiver.

It seems that doing good is, for Saint Benedict, a coldblooded act: something done in cool deliberation and not impetuously or without thinking. It is an act done in the context of Christ, mindful of his words and example, and freely choosing to follow the path he has laid out before us, earnestly praying that the good work that he has begun in us and in others may be brought to completion when its time has come.

In this way, [Christ] who has been pleased to count us in the number of his sons will not ever be grieved by our evil deeds.

What shines forth from this verse is the fact that for Saint Benedict morality is not an abstract ethical code; it is a matter of relationship—our relationship with Christ. Each choice that we make has a bearing on this relationship: either it will strengthen it or it will weaken it. Nothing is indifferent. We live in the presence of Christ. Nothing that we do is without significance for the quality of our side of the relationship. In the final judgment, Christ will say to us, "As long as you did it for the least of these little ones you did it for me."

Imagine going on an outing with a friend who, for no apparent reason, is petulant and abusive to all whom you encounter, who is demanding and difficult to please. Surely the relationship would be weakened and not strengthened by the time spent together. This is the image that Saint Benedict puts before us. We live in Christ's presence, let us act as Christ would act. We who live constantly in Christ's presence need, as it were, to be on our best behavior, to show ourselves worthy of the one who has chosen us and admitted us into his inner circle. This means that often we have to check those actions that come from raw emotion and to stand back and assay everything that we do to see whether it is worthy of Christ.

This is very much in line with the sort of behavior that Saint Benedict talks about later in the Rule when he is discussing the first step of the ladder of humility. This asks of us that we be serious about the commitment we made to Christ, trying to allow it to influence our lives in all their details, avoiding inconsistency between what we profess with our mouths and what we express in our actions. It requires a large measure of vigilance on our part, making sure that, while we have the opportunity, no occasion for doing good and for bolstering the Christ-life within us is disregarded, no matter how small. "Quantitative judgments do not apply."

Such integrity was often described in the monastic tradition by the expression taken from the Beatitudes: "purity of heart." This means a heart that is free of interior conflicts, a will that is single, undivided, and constant. In fact the whole ascetical struggle, as foreseen by Saint Benedict, was concerned with growth in this interior simplicity, not so much through rigorous discipline as by sustained contact with the God of simplicity—the one God who imparts to all who come close the qualities of unity, harmony, peace.

This pervading sense of interior peace is not something that happens quickly, but it is prepared through years of practice, through the long struggle against interior multiplicity and the search for singleness of purpose and the harmony of thought, word, and action. In monastic tradition, every candidate is asked, "What are you seeking?" The same question may well be addressed to each one of us, whatever our state of life, on every occasion. What are you seeking? What goal are your pursuing as you make this choice? How will this course of action contribute to your ultimate happiness? For Saint Benedict, as for so many spiritual masters, living a spiritual life is mostly a matter of viewing all that we do and all that happens to us in the light of eternity.

We do not struggle alone: we take up our arms in the service of Christ who accompanies us in our spiritual warfare and, if we permit it, leads us to victory. By following his captaincy, listening to his voice, and fulfilling his instructions, we will come to that fullness of life that we can never achieve if we rely only on our own energies and insights.

It is worth noting that in this verse appears Saint Benedict's idea that the monk is called to be the son of Christ. Christ is his Father. The idea of the paternity of Christ is not unknown in the writings of the church fathers and is strong in the Rule of the Master, where the Lord's Prayer is addressed not to God the Father but to Christ himself. The Master writes, "It is [Christ] who, despite our unworthiness, grants us the boldness to call him Father when we say this prayer to him" (RM Thp 7-11). This is a theme about which we will say a little more in our next reflection.

6

Thus we must obey him at all times through his good things in us, so that he will not, in time, disinherit us as an angry father [disinherits] his sons.

There is a story in the life of Saint Benedict written by Saint Gregory the Great. Benedict encountered a hermit who had chained himself to a rock in order to prevent himself from wandering. Benedict's response was not approving: "If you are the servant of God, attach yourself with the chain of Christ, not with one of iron."

This saying illustrates clearly one of the main principles of the Benedictine Rule and of the spirituality that derives from it—"Nothing is to be preferred to the love of Christ." It is this sense of personal dedication to Christ that is at the heart of all that the Rule prescribes for the monk's daily life. In the Rule, Christ is the Lord and Commander-in-Chief. He

is the Father, the Teacher, and the Exemplar, the Shepherd
and the Physician. It is because of Christ's work in the soul
that the monk grows into the fullness to which he has been
called. In a sense, monastic life is simply a structured means
of placing oneself permanently within the ambit of Christ's
operation—allowing oneself to be acted upon, challenged,
changed, transformed over the course of a lifetime.

The picture of an angry Christ disinheriting his sons is
not typical either of the Rule of Benedict or of the Rule of
the Master, where the main attribute of Christ is his loving-
kindness or *pietas*. Christ works on us primarily through the
power of attraction rather than by the threat of punishment.
In Saint Benedict's mind the monk is a son and not a slave;
his service is a work of love and not of fear.

What, then, is to be said about the explicit threat of disinheritance made in this verse? First, the possibility of *dis*-
inheritance can be raised only because we are already the
designated heirs for whom it is only a matter of time before
we enter into the fullness of our inheritance. But there are
conditions, as the final verse of the Prologue will remind us.
If we are to become sharers in Christ's kingdom, we must
consent to be, in this life, sharers in his sufferings. We will
probably not be asked to endure the drama of martyrdom;
our means of uniting ourselves with the humility of Christ is
the practice of patience in the ordinariness of daily life. If we
refuse to die with Christ, the possibility of rising with Christ
vanishes. What we have been promised as children of God
through the grace of baptism is conditional on our living as
children of God through the grace of daily life. As the Rule
of the Master states clearly, "The one who is really a son is
one who is similar to his father not only in appearance but
in the manner of his living" (RM Prol. 14).

Christ is grieved by our evil actions and so is pictured
as angrily disinheriting us, but note this is the punishment
of sons; flogging, imprisonment, and death are more likely

responses to those who are "the most wicked of slaves." This designation from the next verse is perhaps a reference to the parable of the unforgiving debtor in Matthew 18. In comparison, disinheritance is a mild punishment—and it is self-chosen.

Whatever good we do is done by virtue of Christ's gifts to us, "his good things in us." And so the credit for our good works belongs not to ourselves but to Christ by whose gift we are what we are and can do what we can do. The power to do good is given to us; it is only by positive resistance to that power that the good is left undone. Such deliberate withholding of our cooperation is an explicit denial of the Christ-life within us, a rupture of our relationship with Christ, a refusal to act in accordance with our status as graced children of God. By not doing the good of which we are capable, we separate ourselves from Christ and from God.

This obligation to follow Christ's lead "at all times" means that the monk's receptivity of grace can never be turned off. A mere tithe of his time and resources is insufficient. This is an extremely demanding vision of the spiritual life—a full-time occupation with no time off. It is, perhaps, to be understood in terms of Saint Benedict's appreciation of the importance of purity of heart, having a single goal and devoting one's entire energy to pursuing it. We can console ourselves, however, that it is clear from the rest of the Rule that its author is realistic enough not to expect that this will happen any time soon. His picture of the monk who has climbed all twelve steps of the ladder of spiritual ascent is of a man who is so utterly possessed by God that nothing else in life matters—arriving at the same point where the martyrs arrived, where all alike can say with Saint Paul, "For me to live is Christ." But this is the end of a lifelong journey, not the beginning nor even the middle. Meanwhile, we will have to confront many inconsistencies, many failures, and, perhaps, much discouragement. But in the end Christ's grace is usually successful in the long term so that we do arrive at that point where his will, and not our own, becomes paramount at all times and in every season.

Also he will not, as a fearsome Lord, angry because of our evil deeds, hand us over to perpetual punishment like the most wicked of slaves, who were not willing to follow him to glory.

Again Saint Benedict puts before us the prospect of eternal damnation for those who do not make the grade. This is a thought that most of us are unwilling to ponder, and so we tend to hurry along until we find something that smoothes our ruffled feathers. There are even those who slice out of the Rule any passages that they think are "not nice." Such an excision, whether mental or physical, does damage to the integrity of Saint Benedict's vision. Rather, we have to sit with the uncomfortable passages and try to hear what they are saying and to discover what we can learn from them.

Many of us experience a very real difficulty in reading ancient texts because they derive from an intellectual and theological ambience so different from our own. Notions such as heaven and hell, judgment and damnation, the wrath of God, the positive appreciation of "fear of the Lord," and the remunerative aspect of spiritual striving are somewhat foreign to us and mostly distasteful. To us, these themes seem to represent a view of God and of human reality that is far too negative, one that is based on a harsh theology that inspires fear rather than love and that does not belong to the New Testament.

Here we must take a step back. Why do we read ancient texts? Surely it is to sit at the feet of a recognized spiritual master, to listen, and to learn wisdom. Why is it that an ancient teacher still has something to say to us after so many centuries have passed and so much extra knowledge is available to us today? Apart from Benedict's credentials as a man of wisdom and holiness, there is another factor at work. When we enter into genuine dialogue with persons of another generation or another culture, we are often surprised that aspects of reality that seem self-evident to us are completely foreign to their view of the world. Conversely, we find in them insights and attitudes that astonish us; we discover that they sometimes see things more clearly than we do. This is because each culture has its particular and characteristic blind spots, which are revealed only through contact with a different culture that does not have the same prejudices and biases. Someone who comes from an individualistic Western society may be amazed at the different attitude toward community that is typical of a more socially oriented culture, even though in many other ways that other culture may seem somewhat primitive.

Benedict belongs to a different age and a substantially different culture. As a result he has inherited a distinctive view of the world, of the human person, of life in community, of the ways of Christian discipleship. Its value to us is not that it is a better worldview but precisely that it is different from our own implicit philosophy of life. As such it challenges us to see more clearly what may be the limitations in the system of belief and value that we have absorbed in growing up. We do not have to abandon the wisdom inherited from our own culture or the fruit of our own experience. It is a question, rather, of listening to what comes to us from a different culture to complement and enhance what already governs our lives.

So, let us not complain that Saint Benedict is not saying the kinds of things that we want him to say, or that we ourselves would include if we were writing the Rule, but let us listen "with the ear of the heart" to hear what he might say that is different, that comes from a different time and place, that challenges us to view reality afresh.

A case in point is the graphic way in which the doctrine of heaven and hell is presented in the Rule, notably in this verse on which we are reflecting.

Whether we care to place it at the forefront of our awareness or not, we human beings were made with the capacity to experience both good and evil and with the consequent capacity to determine the shape of our future by the choices we make for good or for evil: choosing life or choosing death. The Fourth Gospel reminds us that judgment is largely a do-it-yourself affair. We, by cumulative choices, can deliberately exclude ourselves from what is ultimately life-giving. We have within us the possibility of setting our feet on the path to self-destruction. It is not God who condemns us; we ourselves are—frighteningly—masters of our own destiny. It is not God who disinherits us; we disinherit ourselves. It is not God who sentences us to perpetual punishment, but it is we ourselves who choose the roads that inevitably lead to this destination. If we resist the advances of God's love in this life, there is no solid reason to expect that things will be different in the next. The fear that this possibility evokes is due less to some fearsome quality in God than to the dread eventuality that our power of free choice will be seduced to turn away from what is good and life-giving. It is easy, by concentrating on the immediate and not looking at the ultimate consequences of our choices, to choose to follow a path that will eventually carry us to a place at which we do not want to arrive. The story of the rich man called by Christ who chose to retain his goods and not to follow can also be ours. What happened to him eventually we do not know, except that, having declined the invitation, he went away a sadder man.

Here, as so often in reading ancient texts, we need to be aware of a tendency to misread metaphors and similes and to take them too literally. These figures of speech are meant to illumine a single aspect of the reality they are describing. When I say, "It is raining cats and dogs," only a very stupid person would expect to see small quadrupeds falling from the sky! When the Bible speaks about the anger of God, when Jesus speaks about the fires of Gehenna, when Benedict speaks about God condemning us to perpetual punishment, there is question of figurative speech more than of factual statement. It is a useful way of visualizing and opening to reflection an aspect of reality that is otherwise beyond human conception. There is truth contained in the image, but it is not to be found by mistaking the immediate meaning of the image for the more distant reality to which it points.

Benedict is not writing a treatise on the nature of God, or on the "four last things," but exhorting monks to be active in doing what needs to be done if they are to serve God well. His discourse is at the level of motivation. The purpose of the Prologue is to rouse the monk to energetic and sustained labor as he makes his way to the heavenly kingdom. Certainly he is helped and supported by Christ at every level of his endeavor, but he himself, as an adult human being endowed with free choice, must take some responsibility for its ultimate outcome. It is to prevent the monk from slipping into any easygoing negligence that Saint Benedict keeps reminding him that without positive daily exercise his vocation to follow Christ to glory will be unrealized.

The dynamism to which Saint Benedict refers seems to me a little like the "dead man's lever" that is found in the driver's compartment of some trains. Unless the driver keeps activating this mechanism the brakes will be applied and the train will come to a halt. Our spiritual journey, likewise, will eventually slow and stall unless we keep reactivating it by daily acts in which we positively choose the challenging goal we have set before ourselves and reject the easier paths that lead nowhere.

This verse reminds us that we are called to embark on the exciting adventure of following Christ to glory. The ultimate meaning of our life is to be found not in the journey but in arriving at the destination, which is the entry into eternal life—into a state of unchangeable being that fulfills all our potentiality, which eye has not seen and ear has not heard nor has the human heart been able to imagine its extent. This is what God has prepared for those whom love has inspired to follow Christ on the way to glory.

Now, therefore, let us finally arise. Scripture stirs us up saying, "Now is the hour to rise from sleep."

Saint Benedict's use of the two words I have jointly translated as "finally" seems to indicate that he thinks that we, his readers and disciples, have been dormant for some time. Of course, because this is a motivational text rather than a factual description, this moral sleep is relative rather than absolute. Probably we are not the worst people in the world, nor the least sensitive to spiritual stimulation. But Benedict is saying that compared with the spiritual possibilities that are brought within our range by grace, we are pretty sluggish. So we need to bestir ourselves, to get moving, to allow God's grace to propel us further and faster toward the prospects divine providence has prepared for us.

Anybody who has ever had the duty of rousing another from sleep and urging them to get out of bed knows that their efforts are not welcomed. Deep sleep is often followed by a state of delicious drowsiness in which any sense of urgency is dulled. To the recent sleeper it seems that there is nothing so pressing that it cannot be postponed, at least for a few moments. Very soon this momentary wakefulness curls back upon itself and we are asleep again. No call is resisted and resented so fully as the call to wake up.

So we need not be surprised if we do not want to be stirred into action, especially when we do not know exactly what will be involved. We are being summoned to an unspecified alertness. We are being asked to be prepared for unknown challenges, to say yes to demands that have not yet been made. All of this requires a strong faith in Providence and a firm trust that God never calls us to perform beyond our real limits. And we have to be realistic. Despite my forebodings, I can rise reasonably confident that the heroism demanded of me today will not involve utter disgrace, or torture, or martyrdom, but will simply point me toward small actions that transcend the usual boundaries I impose on my benevolence: a word of encouragement here, a few minutes of solicitous listening there, a helping hand, a gesture of forgiveness or solidarity, a hidden initiative that furthers the common good. Occasions for such tiny acts of heroism will present themselves, but only if, first of all, we are awake and alert to their possibility.

Here we see emerging an emphasis on conscience as a guide to action that became stronger as monastic tradition developed. Although Saint Benedict is writing a Rule that defines the external shape of the monastic day and prescribes any number of concrete actions and activities, he is here calling upon the subjective conscience of each person to complement external regulation by an awareness of further possibilities for doing good and avoiding evil. Keeping the commandments is only the minimum; a fuller righteousness is required. This is the "good zeal" about which Saint Benedict speaks at the end of the Rule. This "good zeal" consists in more than the material fulfillment of all the observances that the Rule prescribes; it means going the extra mile by being on the lookout for further occasions of attaching the will to what is good, of changing our actions to something better than what we intended, of showing love. Simultaneously it is a means of blocking the unexamined impulses of self-will and its ambition to be in control of every situation in which it finds itself. To do better requires vigilance. How many times when we are accused of doing wrong or failing to do something appropriate do we reply with excuses such as, "I didn't know," or "I wasn't aware," or "I wasn't thinking"? The moral challenge passed us by because our conscience was not activated; we were asleep.

In traditional monastic language the great means of ending our complacent slumbers was the sting of compunction. The Latin word *compunctio* means a piercing; it is like sticking a pin in somebody with the purpose of waking them up. Compunction involves a moment of awakening, the first glimmer of enlightenment, the dawning of a new day lived against a different horizon. Saint John Cassian, one of Benedict's principal sources, defines compunction as whatever can "by God's grace waken our lukewarm and sleepy souls" (*Conferences* 9.26). This definition seems to envisage us living our spiritual lives in a slumberous state of half-wakefulness. The grace of compunction is the transition to a state of fuller awareness. The great difference between the saints and the rest of us is that they were spiritually awake more of the time than we are; they were alert to possibilities. It is because they went through life in a state of greater consciousness that they were more conscientious in doing good and avoiding evil. We who stumble through life with many mistakes and omissions admire their saintly deeds but without necessarily realizing that perhaps we could imitate them more closely if our spiritual senses were not so drowsy.

Karl Marx is often quoted or misquoted as saying that religion is the opium of the people. For many of our contemporaries this is true in a way different from what he intended. Large numbers of people are staying away from mainline church services precisely because they do not want to be put to sleep; much organized religion is seen as all too boring. The absence of religion does not necessarily make them more socially aware. An alternative source of desensitization has emerged. Our excitement-prone generation is looking for entertainment, something to distract from the tedium of daily living. Everything has to be presented in an entertaining way: the news, the liturgy, even school textbooks. I suppose you won't continue reading these reflections unless you find them at least dimly entertaining. Furthermore, in a context of spectacular images, loud music, and chemical stimulation there is little scope to be touched either by our neighbor's need or by the promptings of conscience. By creating a miasma of sensory fireworks we effectively block out anything beyond what is sensate: any spiritual perceptiveness, any attention to interiority. Our conscience is deadened by sensory overload and we are little aware of the possibilities that are open to us to create a better world.

Becoming more spiritually aware means moving toward a low-impact environment. The voice of conscience and the words of the Gospel are but a still, small voice in our noisy universe. They are further overpowered by the interior fantasies that form from the residual memories of sensory experience. A lively imagination stirs up the emotions and keeps us from attaining that level of inner tranquility that enables us to attend to the promptings of conscience and to the stirrings of the Holy Spirit. The result is that we are so awake on one level that there is no room for a more interior awakening. Most of us cannot truly listen to another speaking if we are simultaneously watching television, texting on our cell phone, and internally fretting about some imagined grievance. In the same way, we cannot be spiritually aware without turning down the volume of other voices. To be awake and alert spiritually we have to limit the amount of attention we give to other areas.

And, according to Saint Benedict, we have to make a start right away. "Now is the hour to rise from sleep." But, as we shall see, this is good news and not just the prelude to further struggle.

And with eyes wide open to the divinizing light, and with astonished ears, let us hear God's voice crying out to us every day and admonishing us.

The voice of God speaks to us every day, if we have ears to listen. What we hear, if we hear anything, can be a source of challenge to our innate tendency to embrace an easygoing lifestyle. But challenge is not always the way that God deals with us. More often, God draws us to transcend our limits by giving us a taste of what lies beyond the world of sense, stirring up in our hearts a mysterious experience of delight that causes us to drop what we are doing and to look more closely. It is a little like Moses being attracted to the burning bush. We experience something that draws us deeper into its mystery. In fact, this is what the word "mystery" originally meant—something so fascinating that we are drawn to penetrate ever more intensely into its reality.

We are awakened and our eyes are opened by what Saint Benedict calls "the divinizing light." The adjective "divinizing" or "deifying" is often translated today simply as "divine" on the grounds that by the sixth century the original meaning had faded somewhat and the term was used more loosely.

This may be so, but the fact remains that the word describes not an aspect of the light in itself but its impact on those who are touched by it. The light shines not for itself alone but to enlighten those who sit in darkness and the shadow of death. When we rise from our sleep and open our eyes we are touched by the light; we are enlightened and energized. We live. This is the "light of life" about which Saint Benedict will speak in a few verses—the light that enlivens.

At the heart of this image is an anthropological statement. If the light from God is for us the source of life in its fullness, then the more light we receive the more fully alive we are. We were created to enjoy union with God, and our lives will be incomplete if this possibility is excluded. A state of spiritual alertness is the means of enlightenment and enlivenment. By being awake we become more fully alive, more fully human, more fully divine.

There is a profound harmony between the external demands of Christianity and the internal dynamism of the human heart. Christian discipleship asks no more and no less of us than that we become what God intends us to be, that we fulfill the potentiality inherent in our individual nature, that we cease acting a role and allow ourselves to become fully ourselves. What theology terms "sins" are, it seems to me, not primarily offenses against God; they are offenses against ourselves—refusals to act in accordance with our God-given natures. We were made in the image and likeness of God; our most authentic behavior is when we act as God acts, as this has been revealed to us in the words and example of Christ. "Be perfect," he said, "as your heavenly Father is perfect." An impossible task had he not exemplified this perfection in his manner of living! To live as Christ lived is not only to live a fully authentic human life but also to realize as completely as possible our own individual vocation. No doubt this is a very lofty ideal, but it is the purpose of Saint Benedict's Rule to show us how to move closer to its realization in the course of a lifetime: not only to be good, but to become ourselves.

Every day God's light shines upon us and God's voice calls to us. Every day there is the prospect of opening ourselves to the energy that comes from God, the energy that can change our life. For many of us the possibility of ongoing, lifelong conversion is a daunting prospect and so we close our eyes and shut our ears. This self-imposed isolation certainly insulates us from challenge, but it also causes us to run away from a source of happiness. God's light is transforming; God's call is life-giving. God draws us by delight, by allowing us to experience something of the joy that comes from allowing God into our hearts and into our lives. So satisfying is this experience on a very deep level that we desire it more; we begin to seek God more intensely and, by grace, to find God more often—though this happens in progressively more subtle ways.

Saint Benedict wants us to be fully conscious of God speaking to us every day and showing us the way forward. He wants us to open our eyes and to listen with the ear of the heart to the call that can make the difference between a life that is half-asleep and one that is fully alive and on the move.

10

"Today, if you hear [God's] voice, harden not your hearts."

Saint Benedict takes his cue from Psalm 94, which he prescribed to be sung at the beginning of the first liturgical office of the day. Its message is clear: "Today if you hear God's voice, harden not your hearts."

As we have seen, God's light shines upon us every day and God's call invites us to a more abundant life. The problem is that too often we are not on the correct wavelength. We are so concerned with what we are feeling and doing that we do not take the trouble to step back from these immediate preoccupations, and so we are not aware of anything beyond them. Our conscience is mostly blank. Occasional glimmers of something else are quickly swamped by our need to do the things we have to do, and so a lot of our good thoughts and good intentions come to nothing.

This insensitivity is moving toward the state that is described in the Bible as "hardness of heart." The surface of the heart is toughened so that it becomes progressively impenetrable: nothing can get through to it. In the Gospel of Mark Jesus often rebukes his disciples for this: "You do not yet know, you do not yet understand, you have a hardened heart" (Mark 8:17). Good will is there, but it is locked behind closed doors, and so it loses contact with the reality of a changing situation; unless something startling happens, there is little prospect of growth.

In the monastic tradition there are four overlapping causes of hardness of heart: forgetfulness of God, the pursuit of trifles, defective self-knowledge, and, finally, its counterpart, defective self-acceptance.

Saint Benedict addresses the problem of forgetfulness, *oblivio*, in the first step of his ladder of humility. The foundation of the spiritual life is to allow oneself to be vulnerable before God, to demolish the personal and cultural defenses that prevent us from listening with the ear of the heart. To make progress spiritually we have to be proactive in seeking out the paths that lead to life and in responding to the graces that have been given us. A vague passivity will get us nowhere; this is why Saint Benedict uses the metaphor of spiritual warfare: we need to be alert and active. A benign forgetfulness may seem harmless enough, but it is a surefire recipe for stagnation.

A second cause of hardness of heart is using all our energy on things that don't really matter. Switching the metaphor slightly, Bernard of Clairvaux sees spiritual blindness as the result of spending too much time and energy on pursuits of no great significance. The quality of our lives is largely shaped by the choices we make concerning the allocation of time. A monk's life gets its character from the fact that much time is spent in liturgy, in prayer, and in sacred reading. If quiet time, prayer, and reading are slowly drifting away from our daily lives, we should not be surprised if we find ourselves becoming less attentive to God and to ourselves than was formerly the case.

The third cause of hardness of heart is a lack of self-knowledge. If we are spiritually illiterate then we find it hard to read what is happening both in our own depths and in our responses to what happens around us. We lose contact with the voice of God in conscience. As a result we are blind. We live our lives at the behest of others or in obedience to our unexamined tendencies and passions. Because we do not know who we really are, we do not have a clear idea of what sort of actions are truly authentic and life-giving for us. We do not know our highest giftedness, and so we operate at a level that is lower than it should be.

Where there is a lack of self-knowledge there will also be a lack of self-acceptance. This will mean that some aspects of who we are and of our personal history will be ignored, denied, or repressed. Typically this often results in projecting our own liabilities onto others, judging them harshly, and rejecting them. The splinter we see in their lives is the projection of the beam in our own. Such lack of self-acceptance tends to make us unfair toward, hard on, and condemnatory of others, as were the Pharisees in the gospels.

The hard heart is a metaphor for a loveless life characterized by suspicion of others, skepticism about their goodness, and a wide-ranging cynicism. It is the opposite of the open and childlike disposition recommended in the gospels. And if you ask how to combat the tendency to hard-heartedness, the answer is simple: be awake and alert to the call of God that comes to us every day through so many channels, calling us to life.

And again, "Let the one who has ears for hearing, hear what the Spirit says to the churches."

The divine call is a personal summons to closer union with God. It is a personal invitation and, hence, very intimate. It is not, however, something private, destined for one individual alone. It is open to everyone, wherever they are in the highways and byways of life; all are invited to the wedding banquet of eternal life.

It is good to remember that the call to holiness is, as Vatican II asserted, universal. Sometimes, when we put a lot of effort into living the spiritual life, we begin to think that we are the only ones who are trying, that the sun shines on our garden alone. This is wrong. Despite appearances, there are still, as the Lord reminded Elijah, seven thousand who have not bowed their knees to Baal, unnumbered multitudes who seek God and serve God in ways that are invisible to us. Our engagement in the spiritual life is never solitary; we go to God in communion with all those in every time and place who have responded to the divine call.

The call to holiness is collective, and the means to that goal are common. Private revelations are extremely rare and often dubious. There is life for us in what the Spirit is saying to the churches. What is common is also personal. Though

God's word comes to us in many and varied forms, the way forward is marked out for us especially by the Scriptures. The primary source of guidance and energy in the spiritual life is the inspired word of God.

We often find in the lives of the saints that Scripture can sometimes be the trigger of a dramatic conversion. This was what happened in the lives of Saint Augustine and Saint Antony of Egypt and many others. In our own case, since we are already living some sort of spiritual life, the role of Scripture is more subtle. Our contact with God's word renews our hope, consoles us in times of wavering, challenges our complacency, and, in a gentle way, guides us in the work of translating the Gospel message into everyday attitudes and behavior.

The more energy we invest in following the way of Christian discipleship, the more important it is that our deployment of this energy is not misdirected. This means that as we progress in the spiritual life it becomes more and more crucial that our efforts are Spirit-based and not merely the works of the ego, however well disguised. As a consequence, the more we are involved in good works, the more we need to set time aside to listen with the ear of the heart to what the Spirit is saying to the churches.

If I am to be a genuine follower of Jesus who strives to live in accordance with the Gospel, then I need to keep before the eyes of my heart the words and example of Jesus. I need to frequent the gospels, to become so familiar with them that they become part of the very fabric of my being. I am called not just to know the Gospel, but to be the Gospel: to be a living Gospel—a unique and particular embodiment of the Good News to all whom I encounter.

This will happen only if I am proactive in opening the Scriptures and reading the Gospel, regularly, carefully, and with an open heart. Part of the specificity of the life that Benedict prescribed for his monks was the amount of time dedicated each day to sacred reading, *lectio divina*. As far as we can establish, he set aside two or three hours every day for this exercise. If you do the arithmetic, this works out at about one thousand hours every year over a lifetime. Can you imagine what sort of change of attitude would be accomplished by such massive exposure?

Of course, nothing much happens immediately. It is the gradual realignment of beliefs and values that is important. We could apply to *lectio divina* the image that one of the Desert Fathers used of spiritual progress in general. When one of his disciples complained that he was making no headway, the elder sent him to the river for a bucket of water. On his return the disciple was told to pour it over a rock. The process was repeated several times until the disciple asked what was going on. The elder replied, when the water has worn away the rock, then come and ask about indications of progress. One pouring of water achieves nothing, twenty pourings are no better, but over the years constant watering has the capacity to wear down the hardest rock, as so many gorges and canyons reveal. It is only a matter of time and perseverance. So it is with our reading of Scripture. One reading makes no difference, but a lifetime of reading has dramatic results.

Devotion to God's word is not merely a matter of spending time with the Bible. We must be, as Saint James reminds us, not merely hearers of the word but also doers of the word. We need to put into practice the lessons we have learned in the school of Christ, applying them to the unique situations in which our life is lived.

This is where the role of memory is important. We have already seen in the last reflection that forgetfulness of God is one of the causes of spiritual insensitivity or hardness of heart. Not surprisingly, therefore, the remembrance of God, *memoria Dei*, is one of the chief means of growing in goodness, as the whole of monastic tradition attests. Carrying something away from our reading and pondering it in our heart as we go about our daily activities are important components of the traditional practice of *lectio divina*. A short text committed to memory is easily transformed into a short prayer that becomes a small, still point around which our working life revolves: a place to which we can return momentarily to center ourselves and, perhaps, find peace in the midst of busyness.

There is a text in one of the *Conferences* of Saint John Cassian that recommends that each hour and at every moment we keep opening up the soil of the heart with the plough of the Gospel. It is a strong image. It is easy for us to become so immersed in the necessary activities of every day that we become forgetful of God; we lose our sensitivity to spiritual realities. It is as though the surface of the heart closes over and becomes hard. In this state it is less likely to welcome the seed of God's word and to give it a favorable environment to grow and bear fruit. At the level of the heart we have become less receptive of the Good News and, perhaps, even a little resistant. This is why, from time to time, we need to keep opening up the soil of the heart with the Gospel plough, momentarily refreshing our memory of what we have encountered in the course of *lectio divina*, taking a minute to reorient ourselves, to make contact with our center, to refocus.

This ongoing familiarity with God's word enables us to recognize the voice of God more easily, just as a friend understands what someone is saying more quickly than a stranger. This means that our sensitivity to God's speaking in the Scriptures is complemented by a similar sensitivity to God's speaking in the events of life, in "the signs of the times."

A Desert Father from sixth-century Palestine, Dorotheos of Gaza, reminds us that for those who are sincerely committed to doing God's will, there are innumerable channels by which this will can be revealed to us, a small child, for example. He reminds us of the incident in the book of Numbers where God spoke through Balaam's donkey. The implication is that if God can communicate a message through a donkey, any human being can serve as a channel of God's life-giving word. So long as we sincerely want to hear that word.

The spiritual life is not something we devise for ourselves and implement with a massive amount of willpower. It is, rather, a response to God's universal call to holiness, a yielding of control and a willingness to have the Gospel as our guide in doing good and avoiding evil. It comes about by paying attention to what the Spirit has to say to the churches through the Scriptures and in so many other channels that flow through our everyday life.

And what does [the Spirit] say? "Come, children, listen to me; I will teach you fear of the Lord."

What does Saint Benedict consider as a fundamental learning for one who embraces monastic life or for any who are beginning to journey on the spiritual path? This verse tells us that what the Spirit teaches to those who are receptive is "fear of the Lord."

Many of our contemporaries dislike the term "fear of the Lord" because it seems to be a negation of New Testament teaching on fear being replaced by love. Some translators try to soften this apparent harshness by rendering it as "reverence in the presence of God" or something similar. This is only to disguise the problem. Perhaps it is better to go beyond the terminology and reflect on the reality that is expressed by this phrase.

First of all, fear of the Lord does not primarily indicate an attitude of being afraid of God; it is closer to being afraid of ourselves, of our own weakness and inconstancy. Let me give an example. Persons with osteoporosis may be very much afraid of a fall, knowing that the brittleness of their bones will make even a minor accident into something very serious. This is a wholesome fear that is based on an acknowledgment of real fragility. When we speak of "fear of the Lord," we are, in the first place, referring to a kind of caution or care that follows the recognition of the precariousness of our virtue. We acknowledge that without God's ongoing help our efforts at living a spiritual life will be destined for failure.

When Saint Benedict speaks about fear of the Lord as the first step of the ladder of humility, he is making the point that to begin a spiritual life we have to start taking its demands seriously. We cannot expect to make progress by drifting aimlessly and hoping that a vague goodwill is sufficient to advance. As Saint Benedict keeps insisting throughout the Prologue, ongoing effort and perseverance are required. Spirituality cannot be a part-time occupation; it needs to communicate its influence to the whole of life, to be a shaping force in our thoughts and in our words, in what we do and in what we omit to do. Such intensity is, indeed, a very high ideal.

Trying to live our whole life in harmony with the teaching of Jesus begins an important dynamic. The harder we try, the more we become aware of the great distance between the ideal and the reality. We experience the kind of interior dissonance about which Saint Paul speaks in the seventh chapter of the Epistle to the Romans. We sincerely desire holiness, but our behavior lets us down. What we do is inconsistent with what we desire to become. If we are honest with ourselves we will be tempted to abandon the ideal as unrealistic. This is not the solution to our problem; it may offer a temporary relief but the abandoned ideal will almost certainly come back to haunt us later in life. The only way to interior peace and ongoing progress is to recognize the truth that it is by God's grace alone that we can attain the completeness to which we are called.

Fear of the Lord is the result of self-knowledge. When we are conscious of our inherent limits and liabilities, we stand humbly before the Lord, in truthful poverty of spirit, dependent on divine mercy and not on our own merits. Such an attitude is essential for genuine Christian discipleship. When Jesus said, "Without me you can do nothing" (John 15:5), he was not exaggerating. It is not possible to advance far on the road to God without coming to terms with the precariousness of our human condition and without the corresponding experience of ultimate dependence on God. "Fear of the Lord," in the sense of the recognition of our own fragility, is an important precondition for prayer. We approach God, conscious of our own neediness, pleading for God's help so that we may become the kind of person that we were created to be. Without self-knowledge, prayer lacks substance.

It is significant that in monastic tradition, following the Old Testament, fear of the Lord is spoken of as the beginning of wisdom. Fear of the Lord is not a cringing terror that makes us want to hide from God. It is, rather, the right attitude for approaching God: an attitude of reverence and respect on the one hand and, on the other, a certain modesty in self-assertion, an awareness of our condition as creatures, as sinners, and as people who have not yet reached their fullest stage of growth. Fear of the Lord guarantees that our attitudes and approaches to God are truthful and not illusory. In this way, our efforts at spiritual living are progressively freed from self-deception and so become means by which we advance in wisdom, experience, and the capacity for discernment. As we grow in freedom from inconsistency, we are less likely to project our own inner confusion on others, and so we are more likely to read situations clearly, to see things as they are, so that we may be a source of guidance for others. Fear of the Lord really is the fundamental step on the road to wisdom.

The monastery is, for Saint Benedict, "a school of the Lord's service" (RB Prol. 45). It is also a school of wisdom.

This implies that wisdom is something that can be learned, given the right instructors and the willingness to be guided. The monastic authors of the Middle Ages noted that *sapientia*, the Latin term for "wisdom," is closely related to the verb *sapere*, "to taste." The implication they drew from this is that wisdom is nothing more or less than an increasing taste for spiritual realities and for God. We often speak about an "acquired taste" for some foods. What this means is that initially we find a food distasteful but, if we persevere with it, we begin to appreciate its distinctive qualities and develop a taste for what was hitherto strange and exotic. In the same way, when we begin to come face-to-face with the reality of God, as distinct from our immature projections, we experience a certain dread because this new experience of God is not what we expected. It is not the comfortable, sentimental God of our early days but One who is "totally other," One whom we need to relearn. Let it be said, however, that it is not so much God whom we have to relearn but, in fact, ourselves. We have to learn to look upon God from the vantage point of an enhanced self-knowledge. Our more complete knowledge of self leads to a more complete knowledge of God. The "school of the Lord's service" is also a school of wisdom and a school of self-knowledge. Our experience of God becomes more profound as we become more aware that we were made for union with God. The closer we come to God the more fulfilled we are as human beings. If we allow ourselves to drift away from God, we become alienated from our own true selves and more entrenched in our own misery.

It is worthwhile remembering that traditional theology has included fear of the Lord among the seven gifts of the Holy Spirit. This is to say that fear of the Lord is one of the effects of the divine indwelling. The task we embrace in monasticism or in spirituality is to become more aware of this gift and to give it greater scope in influencing our lives. To live "in fear of the Lord"—let me repeat—is not to be afraid of God but to have such a strong feeling for our own need of God that we desire more earnestly that God will stand by us to protect us, to guide us, and to give us energy to complete the journey that, by grace, we have begun. This is the lesson that the Holy Spirit imparts to those willing to receive it.

13

"Run while you have the light of life, lest the darkness of death envelop you."

Fear of the Lord is an incitement to effort. Effort is necessary because, following the Rule of the Master, Saint Benedict sees this earthly life as offering the possibility of reaching a level of spiritual attainment that will stand us in good stead for all eternity. Of course, this result is not just human achievement; it is, rather, the natural outcome of faith and grace, the effect of God's empowering action in our lives.

This verse of the Prologue is an adaptation of the words of Jesus in John 12:35: "For a short time the light is among you. Walk while you have the light so that the darkness may not overtake you." There is here a sense of urgency. It is important to get to where we want to be while it is still daylight; otherwise we will be enveloped in darkness and under threat both of falling and of getting lost. Perhaps we who live in a world where artificial sources of light are abundant do not appreciate the power of the image. In an unlit world, movement is virtually impossible. The daylight we enjoy will most certainly come to an end, and darkness and immobility will follow. That is why it is essential that we make good progress while there is light.

Saint Benedict wants us to come close to God while we are still in the prime of life and not to put our trust in the possibility of a deathbed conversion. Just as he admonishes us in his

chapter on the implements of good works to keep death daily
before our eyes (RB 4.47), here he reminds his disciples that
the present moment is the time for action and it will not last
indefinitely, for, as Jesus said, "the night comes in which no one
is able to work" (John 9:4). The choice of God is most potent
when it is made in the context of many attractive alternatives.
When we reach the point where there is nothing much else
to pursue, then religion is almost the only thing left to us. It
is not so surprising that God is easier to find as the rest of our
life is winding down. We choose God simply because there
is nothing else left. Benedict wants us to do more than this.

We will be on earth only for a short time; as the psalmist says, "seventy years or maybe eighty for the vigorous" (Ps
89:10). If we are going to make an impact on the world, or
even if we are going to clean up our own act, then we need
to get started right away, "for the night is coming in which
no one is able to work." "Run while you have the light of life,
lest the darkness of death envelop you."

The word "run" is a significant word for Saint Benedict.
It occurs four times in the Prologue and twice elsewhere in
the Rule. Running is a much more energetic activity than
walking. It is indicative of enthusiasm. The sad and the weary
do not run; they drag themselves along, as though uncertain
that the next step is possible. Those who are truly touched
by grace cannot contain themselves. Remember that wonderful passage in Isaiah: "Boys tire and become weary and
youths stumble, but those who hope in the Lord renew their
strength; they get wings like those of eagles, they run and do
not become weary, they walk and do not tire" (Isa 40:30-31).

A strange dynamic can be observed in monastic life and,
I suppose, wherever the spiritual life is lived intensely. In the
natural order it is the young who are strong and have a great
capacity for action; this vigor declines as they reach middle
age and pass beyond it until, in the end, all is weariness.
One who has fully embraced the way mapped out by Saint

Benedict will experience the reverse of this process. Sluggish beginnings will eventually give way to a greater level of involvement until, as the monk internalizes more and more of the values inherent in his vocation, he begins to experience a level of fervor hitherto unknown to him. Natural energies decline; spiritual energies increase.

Saint Bernard of Clairvaux characterizes this development under three headings: *disciplina, natura, gratia.* First, a person passes though a learning phase, being trained through external structures and the overt guidance of others. Then, as the values inherent in these practices begin to be internalized, the practices themselves become second nature, performed with relative ease and without resistance. Finally, instead of being an external imposition, the way of life becomes a source of deep gratification. It is not the practices that have changed; they have remained more or less the same over the decades. What has changed is the human heart, which has been molded by the practices in such a way that "what was formerly observed fearfully, [the monk] now begins to keep without any labor, naturally from habit; no longer from any fear of hell but for love of Christ, from good habit and from delight in [the practice of] the virtues" (RB 7.68-69). The heart has been enlarged by years of faith-filled practice so that the monk now "runs along the road of God's commandments with the indescribable sweetness of love" (RB Prol. 49). Monastic life is not meant to be drudgery. It is, rather, the work of enthusiasm.

There is another aspect to running. Apart from professional runners, health runners, and those who are always late, it is mostly children who run. They run out of sheer exuberance, because walking seems too staid to serve as a vehicle for their vitality. There is in running an overflowing happiness that cannot be contained in a slower pace. This is the image Saint Benedict proposes when he recommends that his disciples run: childlike simplicity, as in the gospels; happiness; vitality. There is, in such a spirit, a degree of intensity that some of us are fearful to embrace. Western society is renowned for its permissiveness, but there are some activities that are disallowed—being intense about God is one of them. We often try to hide our religious fervor, as though it were something of which we ought to be ashamed. Fearful of being identified with the phony facades of televangelists and others, we retreat into our shells and avoid anything that possibly could be perceived as ostentatious.

This modesty is a healthy instinct, but it can be carried too far. By our baptism we are also called to be witnesses of the grace we have received—not necessarily by speaking but by our gracious manner of living. This is certainly true of monasteries, where extreme fidelity to the Gospel is publicly proclaimed, but it should be true also in the lives of all Christ's followers. By running on the road of discipleship with fervor and enthusiasm, we affirm in the sight of all that we believe there is more to life than what can be perceived by the senses and known by reason. We are called to be witnesses to the reality of the spiritual world. This is our task. In God's providence it may be that others will catch fire from our flame.

Meanwhile, it is the time to start training, to get ourselves into condition so that we may be able to run with fervor along the road that leads to eternal life.

14

And the Lord, seeking his workman in the midst of a multitude of people, cries out to him and says:

The initiative and impetus of the monastic enterprise comes entirely from God. Otherwise it will lead nowhere.

God calls some to engage more intensely in the spiritual pursuit. It seems that not everyone experiences this attraction, and not everyone who feels so called is inclined to respond positively. All spiritual life is a response to the initiative of God "who loved us first." We seek God only because God first sought us, calling out to us in the midst of a multitude. Far from being an imposition or a burden, it is a great privilege to be called and a great gift of grace to be able to respond.

To what are we called? In Saint Benedict's view the monk is called to be a worker. This is a return to a theme that we have often encountered in the course of these reflections. The Rule emphasizes that sincerely living a spiritual life takes a lot of effort. We are not called merely to be spectators of the work God accomplishes in us; we are summoned to active participation. We are called to work hard to ensure that the grace of God is not poured out in vain.

This is the mysterious dynamism with which Saint James grapples in his Epistle. The only way that we can determine whether faith or vocation is genuine is to observe whether the fruits of faith or vocation are brought forth. A good tree yields good fruit. Authentic faith cannot exist unless, in love, it gives birth to the good works that are the outward expression of inward faith. Likewise, the sense of vocation is verified only when it leads to a practical living out of the values of that vocation, not only for a short time, but over many years and through many difficulties and reversals of fortune.

If the monk is envisaged as a worker, then the monastery is his workshop. This is explicitly stated by Saint Benedict at the end of his fourth chapter where he speaks about the implements of the monk's trade: good works. This is a thought-provoking way of speaking about monasticism and, I suppose, it can refer also to all spiritual life. The bread-and-butter basis of monastic life is the workmanlike performance of whatever good deeds a particular situation demands. So, following chapter 4, a definition of a good monk should go something like this: A good monk is one who loves God and neighbor, who does not murder, commit adultery, or steal, and so on for the remainder of the seventy-four good works that Saint Benedict enumerates.

It is hard enough to remember a list as long as this, much less to make it a daily priority to put them all into practice. Staying with the image of a workman and his tools is helpful. In the normal course of events, a worker uses only one tool at a time; when its task is finished he puts it down and takes up another to accomplish the next stage of the process. In the same way, we will probably not have to struggle implementing all seventy-four of Benedict's injunctions simultaneously, but on any given day or week or year, there may be one or two that need to be taken especially seriously. Tomorrow the spiritual task may require of me a different kind of intervention.

It will make a lot of difference in the attitude of a prospective monk if he sees himself as one called to be a worker and not merely a recipient of the blessings the monastery has to offer. It can sometimes happen that a person enters a monastery with the unformulated notion of receiving great benefits from this step; there is an expectation that the monastery will provide an enrichment of his life rather than make demands on his time and energy. Of course, when monastic life fails to fulfill these rosy expectations, there is a great sense of disillusionment; the young man begins to see himself as a victim and even a martyr and may eventually withdraw from the community.

Saint Benedict is saying to such a one, "You are coming to the monastery, you are engaging in the spiritual art, not to receive something, but to give whatever you have. This endeavor will provide you with the opportunity to use your highest gifts in the service of something larger than yourself. You are called to be a worker, to give of your talents with disinterested generosity, to labor much in the service of the Lord and for the benefit of others. You are not the center of the universe; you are a worker. You are a valued worker and your unique task is significant in the context of the whole, but first you have to learn your craft in all its aspects. Come into the workshop and see the array of implements here. With some of these you will be already familiar; there are others that you must learn to use. Skill with them requires the willingness to accept instruction and learn, and the patience to practice for a long time until you become proficient in the various implements of the spiritual craft."

To see oneself as a simple member of the monastery's workforce, engaging with others in the works of asceticism and worship, is to lay a solid foundation for acquiring humility. Instead of a self-preening solitary performance, I am doing no more than many others. If I am sincere in my self-scrutiny, I will probably come to the conclusion that those around me are doing much better than I. We will begin to make our own the words that Jesus puts in the mouth of a diligent worker: "I am an unprofitable servant, doing no more than is due from me" (Luke 17:10).

God's seeking of a workman reminds us of the parable of the workers in the vineyard. In the first place, God does not call everyone at the same point in their life: some he summons early, others later, and others again at the eleventh hour. This is because the initiative for the monastic or spiritual journey is from God and not from us. Second, the labor demanded of each varies in degree: some are obliged to work harder than others. Third, the payment for the work done is out of all proportion to the energy expended in doing it. "Eye has not seen, nor ear heard, nor has the human heart conceived what God has prepared for those who love him" (1 Cor 2:9; RB 4.77).

Many people have romantic or idealistic notions about monastic life that are untrue. The image of the monk as a

workman is a reminder that monastic life is not an idyllic existence but rather something ordinary, obscure, and laborious.
The same is true of the spiritual life in general. By taking the
Gospel seriously, we are not joining a privileged elite that can
afford to take life easy, relying on God's grace to do everything. We are committing ourselves to the serious pursuit of
self-knowledge, the practice of virtue, and the abandonment
of all arrogance and laziness. This is hard work, as any know
who have tried it. It is even harder to keep at it year after
year, decade after decade, for a lifetime, but this is what the
Lord asks of us. It is to such labor that we are called.

"Who is the person who wants life and desires to see good days?"

At this point Saint Benedict, closely following the text
of the Rule of the Master, begins to offer a reflection on the
text of Psalm 33, in much the same way as I am reflecting on
what he wrote. We find a similar use of the same verses of the
psalm in 1 Peter 3:10-12. This citation is another reminder,
first, of the importance of Scripture in the formulation of
a monastic philosophy of life and spirituality and, second,
that Scripture will often guide us on our way not so much
by giving us ready-made answers but by asking questions
and inviting us to find their answers in our own experience.

The psalm begins by calling to us, "Come, children, listen
to me and I will teach you the fear of the Lord." So we are
going to learn what fear of the Lord is. It is desiring eternal
life, controlling our tongue, living moral lives, seeking peace,
and living in the presence of God. And so, first of all, we are

invited to ask ourselves, "Am I the sort of person who is truly seeking the fullness of life and happiness?" and to hear what answer to this question resounds in the depths of our hearts.

The work to which God directs us is not an external task waiting for someone to come along and do it. It is not as though God has a roster of duties with a name placed beside each one of them. The work God gives us is not primarily determined by external factors. The work of God is to bring to actuality all the potential inherent in our individual human nature. We are not so much called to do as to become. Our primary God-given task is to become the person whom God has called into being.

The energy of our Christian and monastic vocation derives from inherent desire. This is not the kind of desire or lust that follows our seeing something that pleases us and then wanting to possess it. This sort of desire makes its object into a commodity, whether it is directed to a person, a thing, a skill, some level of social status, or even an opportunity to do good. We see something or hear about it and we begin consciously to desire it. Of course, this process happens all the time and it is not necessarily a bad thing; its moral quality is determined by the object. To desire that harm befall a rival is clearly a bad desire. To desire that a friend be cured of cancer is a good desire, though it may be ineffectual. To desire food when one is hungry is a natural desire and, therefore, good. These are desires that depend on what we see and hear and feel; we would not have experienced these desires if we had not first become aware of the situations that triggered them.

The desire about which we are speaking goes deeper than the various desires that ripple across the surface of our life. It preexists our awareness of it. It is embedded in our being from the very beginning, but it manifests its presence only later in life and spasmodically. This is a desire that we do not share with the animal kingdom. It is a movement of our being beyond ourselves and beyond the world of which we are a part into a transcendent reality that we cannot fully perceive, understand, or describe. So it is a mysterious yearning that is planted in the human heart that has no clear object. It is an invitation to a journey, the destination of which is unknown. It begins from where we are, but we do not clearly know where it is going or by what road we must travel to arrive where we desire to be.

Christians term this longing at the deepest level of our being a desire for God. Many are familiar with the sentiment addressed to God by Saint Augustine at the beginning of his *Confessions*: "You have made us for yourself, and our hearts are restless until they rest in you." What this indicates is that human beings, created in the image and likeness of God, cannot be entirely defined in terms of our earthly origin and function. There is a spark of divine fire in us that causes us to look beyond the earthly sphere for the fulfillment of our deepest yearnings. Nothing in space and time can satisfy us fully and permanently. Every desired gratification quickly loses intensity and fades, and something else, equally imper-manent, is sought to takes its place. As Teresa of Avila wrote, "All things are changing; only God changeth never."

Sometimes the first sign of a more conscious desire for God comes about through an experience of disillusionment or dissatisfaction. We say, "There must be more to life than this." It is a common experience that God seems to be more easily found in times of trouble and disturbance than when everything is going well and we are living at the top of the world. Routine and habit can so control our lives that our perception of ultimate realities is dulled. It is only when something happens—either externally or internally—that the shell is cracked and we begin to look beyond what is immedi-ate and familiar. We become searchers for "something more."

It is this instinct to leave behind immediate gratifications and become pilgrims of the Absolute that opens us to the possibility of a more spiritual life and, maybe, leads us to the monastery. Human beings are pilgrims by their very nature. One who seeks no further than the comforts of this life is not much more than a spiritual vegetable; something is lacking in that person's humanity. This basic instinct to spirituality may be hardwired or it may be simply the effect of the universal frustration at having dreams and ideals larger than the possibility of realization. Not every spirituality becomes religion, and not every religious response to life takes the form of an organized institution, so we cannot equate this generic spiritual instinct with a belief in God or the membership of a specific religious body. The instinct itself is deeper than conscious understanding and external belonging. It operates at the level of being; it is the result of our God-given nature. Such desire consists essentially in a restless search for a reality beyond what is tangible and visible, a search that makes us human.

This primal desire is what generates in us the interest and energy to begin a spiritual or monastic journey. We cannot always explain it logically; it is just there. If we want to persevere in our quest, then we must remain in contact with this basic drive, to allow ourselves to become ever more conscious of it and to look to it for direction. As the author of the fourteenth-century mystical work *The Cloud of Unknowing* wrote, "Let this thing lead you and guide you wherever it wants." This desire for God exists deep within us, at the level of being; we need to bring it up to the level of consciousness so that it may become a more potent force in the ordering of our life.

Perhaps this is why many monastic rituals of initiation begin by asking the candidate, "What do you seek?" What brings you to take this radical step? Similarly, of Saint Bernard of Clairvaux his first biographer wrote that he used to address to himself the words of the Gospel: "Why have you come to this place?" What is happening here is not neurotic self-doubt but an invitation to go deeper than surface motivations to discover what is really pushing us in the direction that we are going. What is it that makes us want to follow the spiritual path when so many others—maybe even our closest friends—see no point in what we are doing?

It is probably true for many of us that we are unable to provide a logical explanation for the most significant, life-changing choices that we have made in the course of a lifetime. We can only demonstrate that the decisions were not totally irrational, and we can offer supporting arguments. Such statements, although sincere, are often no more than public relations; they attempt to explain something that transcends the boundaries of logical explanation. They are fig leaves inadequately concealing the fact that the choices we made came from deep inside and bear little relationship to the world of common sense and practicality.

There is something profound within human nature that longs for a life that the world cannot give or sustain; it yearns for that fullness of vitality and happiness that the New Testament calls "eternal life." This is real life, no longer divided into mutually exclusive parts and spread over decades, but concentrated in a single point of intense existence. This is the "more abundant life" that Jesus came to communicate to us. This alone is the complete fulfillment of the potentiality of human being. The question Saint Benedict asks us is simple, "Is this what you want?"

16

If hearing this, you respond, "I do," the Lord says this to you.

It is fairly clear that God forces no one to do good and avoid evil. The road to life beckons us, but no progress can be made until we positively choose to take that road and advance along it. This is a step that many of us are reluctant to take. The freedom to choose can easily cast us into a state of anxiety, particularly when it is a question of multiple and mutually exclusive options.

We love making choices about things that do not matter much. Supermarkets play up this attitude by offering us many differently packaged versions of virtually the same product. Multiple channels of television permit us to hop from one to another so that we do not have to stay with a particular program if its dazzle begins to fade for us. We can surf the internet for the rest of our lives without ever coming to the end of strongly held yet contradictory opinions on every topic under the sun. There is no end to the frivolous choices with which we are bombarded every day of our life.

We are much less comfortable with choices that are more serious. We live in a time when many people, young people especially, are fearful about making commitments and are often quite cavalier about commitments already made. Experimentation is OK, a temporary arrangement is OK, but taking something on for the long term, or even for a lifetime, is frightening. We are extraordinarily open to new experiences on condition that we can terminate them at will and start something else. We do not want to burn our bridges. Passing a point of no return seems too risky for many.

There are, however, many avenues of life that require of us at least long-term commitment. To be a brain surgeon or a concert pianist is impossible without a huge investment of resources: money, time, energy. The fifteen minutes of fame garnered by Olympic athletes is purchased by years of training, serious sacrifices, and, often, many injuries. It is foolish to think that in the altogether more important area of making a success of our life we can make progress without effort and perseverance. Without a firm, stable, and long-lasting act of the will, we will not go anywhere.

This is why Saint Benedict wants us to give overt assent to the proposition of making a spiritual or monastic journey. "Are you one who longs for life; what is your answer?" Later on in the Rule when he speaks about the admission of newcomers to the monastery, Saint Benedict shows that he practices what he preaches. Far from being an enthusiastic recruiter who lures into the monastery everyone who crosses his path, he wants to slow the whole process down so that the man considering monastic life has a chance to think through what he is about to undertake and to look at it from every angle.

Those charged with formation are instructed to make sure that the aspirant is formally told about all the "hard and harsh things" that await him as he journeys towards God. There is no cover-up here! No dismissal of apprehensions with breezy optimism! Saint Benedict wants the whole Rule to be read to the candidate three times during the period of probation so that he has a clear idea of the nature of the life he is about to embrace. Each time the trainee monk hears the words, "This is the Rule under which you wish to serve; if you can observe it, enter; if not, go away a free man" (RB 58.10). There is no compulsion here. Likewise, at the end of the period of probation he will have a final chance to discern whether to embrace a commitment that will bind him for the rest of his life: "And if, after reflecting within himself, he promises to keep everything and to obey all that is commanded him, then let him be received into the community, knowing that it is established by the law of the Rule that from that day he will not be allowed to go out from the monastery nor to withdraw from the yoke of the rule which, after so much reflection, he could have refused or accepted" (RB 58.14-16).

Saint Benedict is not interested in a quick burst of initial enthusiasm that quickly burns itself out when confronted with the reality of everyday challenges. Stability is one of the fundamental values of Benedictine spirituality. Once we begin something we stay with it until the process is complete—whether it is a question of reading a book all the way through from beginning to end (RB 48.15), remaining constant during the process of initial formation (RB 58.9), or faithfully practicing all the virtues throughout one's entire life (RB 4.78).

Stability is a result of an enduring act of the will giving assent to God's grace. An enduring act of the will is the result of making a choice of high quality. A high-quality choice presupposes that we slow down to make time for reflection, discernment, and, probably, counsel. When the decision to continue the journey is sound then commitment follows. Those of us who are human and not angels will not always live up to our commitments. We will often be tempted to do things that are inconsistent with the fundamental direction of our lives. We will sometimes allow bad habits to take root in us that create anxiety and consume our energy. If, however, there is a central commitment to monastic life or Christian discipleship such incidental wanderings will not destroy us. They will certainly slow our journey. These compromises to our integrity will cause us to experience an uncomfortable degree of disappointment and frustration at our lack of progress. But so long as our core commitment remains substantially intact, there will be within us a constant invitation to return from our wanderings. Like the Prodigal Son in a distant land, we will hear within us the subtle voice of conscience singing, "Come back to the Father."

Yes, we are those who want life and desire to see good days, but for this desire to bear fruit we must be willing to walk the narrow road that leads to life. Many want life; only few choose life. There is a difference. To choose life involves implementation at a practical level. Discipleship is more than wistful thinking. In Saint Benedict's view, it is effort, it is struggle, and it is spiritual warfare. If you choose to make seeking God the foundation of your life, then there will be hard practical choices to be made every day. Some of these

Saint Benedict raises in the next few verses; others he will bring to the fore as he describes, in the seventy-three chapters of the Rule, the life that he wants his disciples to lead.

"If you want to have true and perpetual life, forbid your tongue from evil and your lips lest they speak deceit. Turn away from evil and do good. Seek peace and pursue it."

The life to which we are called is described by Saint Benedict as "true and perpetual" or "authentic and permanent." He is speaking about the life that follows our time on earth and for which the practice of monasticism is meant to prepare us. Living a spiritual life and, even more so, living a monastic life make no sense if their meaning is sought only in terms of earthly existence. As Saint Paul says, "If for this life only we have hope in Christ Jesus then, of all people, we are the most to be pitied" (1 Cor 15:19). Monastic life is a preparation for heaven; if there is no afterlife, then the whole business is pointless.

How are we to prepare ourselves for a life that "eye has not seen nor ear heard nor has it entered into the human heart to conceive" (1 Cor 2:19)? Well, the first step is easy to understand but exceedingly difficult to practice. Adopting the response given to the question by Psalm 33, Saint Benedict tells us to begin to change the tone of our lives by exercising control over our speech. "Forbid your tongue from evil and your lips lest they speak deceit."

It is a readily observable fact that good religious people rarely commit murder, adultery, or lapse into idolatry. In gen-

eral their behavior meets or even surpasses common standards. Where they often fall down is in the area of speech. In
what they say they can be judgmental, violent, and positively
nasty; they can use speech dishonestly, to cover up their own
failings, and to present a deceitful image to the world. Their
lives are not transparent. Language serves the purpose of fig
leaves to cover the nakedness of who they are.

It is as though good people are resentful of having to lead
good lives and envy those who live otherwise. Their apparent
goodness can be merely the result of social constraint or a
tyrannical superego. It is not fully sincere. The heart remains
unconverted. And even though such people are careful not
to cross the line into sinful actions, by their words they give
vent to the passions that, in the seventh chapter of Saint
Mark's gospel, Jesus taught reside deep inside every person.
They kill, hurt, harm, and plunder with their words, while
retaining the semblance of innocence in their actions. The
third chapter of Saint James' Epistle addresses this problem
very directly: "All of us fall in many ways. If anyone does not
fall by word, that person is perfect" (Jas 3:2).

This is one of the reasons why Saint Benedict sees the
practice of silence as important in monastic life. Without
control of speech, it is likely that unwholesome attitudes are
expressed and reinforced, attitudes that are inconsistent with
the high ideals we have embraced in following the spiritual
or monastic path. Gossip, murmuring, backbiting, and verbal
attack gradually undermine community spirit and lead to unnecessary suffering for ourselves and others. Following Saint
James's image of the rudder (Jas 3:4-5), we may say that our
whole life follows the lead of the tongue. Unholy speech leads
to unholy attitudes that, in due course, will be expressed in
unholy behavior. It is as simple as that.

In our speech as in our whole life the most fundamental
moral principle is, as the psalm continues, "Turn away from
evil and do good." There are two complementary paths that

we may take if we wish to upgrade our lives. We can concentrate either on avoiding evil or on doing good. These two options are merely two ways of looking at the same reality. The important word in this line is really "and." It is not enough to turn away from evil since we may well sin by omission; we must also do good. It is not enough merely to do good; it may be that there are sinful areas in our lives that we are not facing. Instead of uprooting bad habits, we attempt to cover them over with a proliferation of good works. No. We are called both to "turn away from evil and do good."

We do not practice morality in a hermetically sealed chamber, where everything that happens is under our control and predictable. We are called to do good and avoid evil in a wild world where we do not know what challenges or temptations we will meet on any given day. When I wake up in the morning I do not know what each day will bring. Will something happen that will cause me to lose my temper? Will I give vent to a long-standing antipathy through harsh and unfair words? Will I succumb to gluttony, lust, or jealousy? Will I meet a situation to which I will be able to respond with heroic generosity and love? Who knows what is ahead of me? Who knows whether today will mark a new beginning in my life, for better or worse? Morality is not a rigid system that removes all risk or adventure from our lives. It involves staying alert at all times and responding to every upcoming event in the light of my fundamental ideals and values.

Today I am called by grace deliberately to turn away from evil and knowingly and willingly do good. If I respond positively to that invitation then I am walking, or even running, along the road that leads to eternal life. If I decide to put my conversion off until tomorrow, then already my spiritual life is starting to stagnate.

In this verse of the Prologue, Saint Benedict proposes three creative avenues to pursue: control of the tongue, basic morality, and, finally, peacemaking.

As anyone knows who is familiar with monasteries following the Rule of Saint Benedict, their watchword is *pax* or peace. Peace is what everybody wants. They want it so badly, as Saint Augustine wryly noted, that sometimes they go to war to achieve peace. But wanting peace and pursuing peace are not necessarily the same thing. In the Beatitudes, Jesus declared blessed those who made peace, the peacemakers. Peacemaking is not such an easy task; it requires many other virtues. We cannot make peace in ourselves or in the community to which we belong unless we are humble, meek, and patient. As many of those who have served in the United Nations peacekeeping forces understand, keeping the peace is a dangerous occupation.

Peace is more than the absence of disturbance. Peace is not a blanket thrown over dissonant elements to cover up their fighting. Peace, as Bishop Helder Camara wrote once, is not the silence of a stagnant swamp. It is not the absence of activity. Peace cannot be separated from justice, from morality, from the proactive reconciliation of opposites. Peace is, according to Saint Augustine's definition, "the tranquility of order." If there is peace in a monastery, it is not because the monks are drugged into quietude by the "opium of the people," but because there is good order: priorities are observed and the law of charity and forgiveness prevails. Social peace and interior peace both depend on submission to the will of God, trust in Providence, and a firm faith that "God can write straight on crooked lines." You might remember the episcopal motto adopted by Angelo Roncalli before he became Pope John XXIII: "In God's will is peace." When we live in harmony with God's will, then our tongues are under control, we live good lives, and our hearts and minds are possessed by the tranquility of good order; we are in a situation where growth is possible. This is the peace "that surpasses understanding," the peace that is the Lord's gift to those who are his true disciples.

18

"And when you have done this, my eyes will be upon you and my ears [will be attentive] to your prayers. Before you call upon me I shall say to you, 'Here I am.'"

Having set forth the conditions for a good life, the psalm continues with its result. "The eyes of the Lord are upon the righteous." The Rule of the Master changes this a bit, making it "you righteous." Saint Benedict, fearing that the reader might become complacent and puffed up, changes it again and says simply, "My eyes will be upon you and my ears [will be attentive] to your prayers."

The message is crystal clear. To the extent that, by God's grace, we upgrade our lives, God comes closer to us. We begin to experience God's benevolent gaze following us wherever we go, whatever we do. We are not alone. Even our most interior struggles are conducted with God watching and supporting us.

There is a text is Isaiah (Isa 59:2) that spells out the opposite of what Saint Benedict is saying: "It is your iniquities that have separated you from your God; your sins have hidden his face from you, so that he will not hear." Apart from the damage wrought on ourselves, on others, and on the world, our sins also have the effect of creating a barrier between us and God so that God seems so distant that we cannot make contact. We call out and God seems not to answer, since we are unable to hear any response. Our sinfulness has the effect of making us spiritually blind and deaf. We can see and hear what comes to us through our senses, but the invisible world of God is a closed book to us.

According to John Cassian, all the various exercises of monastic life are intended to bring us to a state of purity of heart. This is to say that the active phase of our spiritual journey reduces the level of inconsistency in our life and helps us to come to a point of simplicity, singleness of purpose, an undivided heart. No longer is there constant interior warfare between good and less good impulses, but our natural tendency to the good is progressively enhanced and strengthened so that it becomes easier for us to live in accordance with the ideals we profess.

The effect of this interior simplicity is that the self becomes transparent; it becomes like a window that the divine radiance easily penetrates and so lights up all that is within. If we lack purity of heart, the window of the soul is covered with dirt; light penetrates only feebly and all within exists in a state of continual obscurity.

Immoral or inconsistent behavior erects a barrier between us and God, because it degrades the powers of the soul. Interior division incapacitates us. Living a spiritual life in this state is like attempting to run the one hundred–meter sprint in the Olympics wearing a wet overcoat. An ongoing habit of sin is a burden that slows us down, demoralizes us, and makes us want to abandon the journey. We are aware only of our own struggle; we have lost sight of the goal; we have lost sight of God.

The Old Testament often refers to this unhappy state by using the image of God hiding his face. It seems that God has lost interest in us and no longer supports us, although the reality is that it is we who are the impedance. We have lost interest in maintaining our own integrity and our lives are full of compromise and rationalization. As Saint Augustine laments, God is near to us but we are far from God. Like Adam and Eve, after their fall from grace, we hide from God and try to cover our shame with excuses and clever words. It is we who hide our face, not God.

Benedict is calling us to greater purity and probity, promising us that if we strive to live better lives then God will become more present to us. We are being advised by God's grace to clean the windows of our soul and then things will start happening. We become conscious of living under the benevolent gaze of our heavenly Father and that God is always ready to listen to our prayers. We must insist. The change is in us not in God. God is always present and listening, but our consciousness of that reality often fades and is sometimes extinguished.

So willing is God to hear us that Saint Benedict attributes to God these words: "Before you call upon me I shall say to you, 'Here I am.'" This is a quotation from Isaiah 58:9: "Then you will call, and the LORD will answer; you will cry for help, and he will say: 'Here am I.'" Our text changes the quotation by adding the idea that God is ready to answer before we begin to call out. This seems to be a reminiscence of a later text, Isaiah 65:24: "And it will come to pass that before they cry out to me I will hear them and while they are still speaking I will hear." The eagerness of God to respond to our prayer is a wonderful image. It is also the reality. If we are less than fully aware of the goodness and kindness of God, it is because our spiritual senses have been dulled by too many compromises. If we clean up our act, everything will seem different.

19

What is sweeter for us, dearest brothers, than this voice of the Lord inviting us?

The concept of sweetness evoked in this verse may come as a surprise to us. The thesaurus gives the following as equivalent meanings for "sweet": sugary, syrupy, saccharine.

These do not seem like words that we would normally associate with the thought of Saint Benedict, whom we may perceive as moving more in the direction of good order, duty, austerity, and unemotionality.

This apparent dissonance gives us all the more reason to look closely at what this verse is expressing. God's voice is not that of the thunderous dictator of the Decalogue on Mount Sinai, compelling us to restrain our natural impulses and follow, under threat of punishment, an external code of behavior. God's voice became flesh and presented himself as one who was meek and humble of heart, who ate with the marginalized and with sinners, and who invites us all to come to the eternal banquet. This is not a fearsome voice but a voice of love and acceptance. This still, small voice is not easily heard amid tumult and struggle, but when it is sensed, it is perceived as a force of immense attraction that draws and energizes and delights.

In the spirituality of Saint Augustine, which influenced Saint Benedict, the idea of God drawing us by delight was very important. Once the reality of Christ is perceived, there is an almost-instinctive movement of the heart and mind toward him: the desire to be with Christ, to be his disciple, to become like Christ. As Saint Augustine wrote,

> "Delight in the Lord who will grant the requests of your heart" (Ps 36:4). There is pleasure for the heart of one for whom the heavenly bread is sweet. If the poet was able to say, "Each is drawn by his own desire"—not by necessity but by pleasure, not by obligation but by delight—how much more strongly must we say that the human being who is drawn to Christ is one who delights in truth, who delights in blessedness, who delights in goodness, who delights in eternal life, all of which Christ is. Can it be so that the bodily senses have their pleasures but the soul has nothing that pleases it? (*In Ioan. Ev.* 26.4)

The delight that we experience when we find ourselves addressed by God, whether through the interior voice of conscience or externally through the Scriptures or the church, is another indication of the fundamental affinity between us and God—our kinship with Christ. Following Christ is what we were made to do; every step we take in this direction is an affirmation of our God-given nature. Just as a drink is delightful when we are thirsty and a rest when we are weary, so the sense of being called by God and invited to follow Christ wakes us from our drowsy half-life and opens before us the abundance of a more complete human existence.

The Lord's call to follow him has an effect on us similar to that which it had on the first disciples. Once we heed the call, we willingly leave behind whatever we are doing and walk with him, wherever he goes. We are not dragging our feet, but walking and running, full of happiness to be called.

This delight has another function; it makes us more motivated to embrace that level of renunciation that following Christ always involves. In the call narratives of the gospel we see the first disciples leaving behind all that was familiar and comfortable and moving in faith into the challenging unknown. Every time we attempt, under grace, to reorient our lives more fully toward God, we find that there is a price to pay. To seize hold of what is better we must let go of what is good. It is only the intensity of the experience of delight in the Lord that can motivate us to turn our backs on what was hitherto an important and meaningful source of gratification. Do you remember the words of Jesus in Matthew 13:44? "The kingdom of heaven is like treasure hidden in a field. One who found it, hid it again, and then for very joy went and sold everything and bought that field." First the person found the treasure and only then, in the fullness of joy and delight, was the necessary renunciation possible.

The renunciation that monastic life and every serious spirituality demand is built on the premise that we have first experienced some attraction beyond the visible world of sense and feeling. It is in pursuit of the delight promised by this transcendent reality that we let go of lesser gratifications and begin our journey. First comes attachment and only then detachment, and not the other way round. In the course of our lifetime we are encouraged to go further by sometimes experiencing again the sweetness of the Lord's ongoing invitation. As the psalmist says, "Taste and see how good the Lord is" (Ps 33:9). Such experiences are more than random collateral benefits. Without returning to such delightful contact with God, at least sometimes, we will quickly become discouraged and lose our sense of direction.

Not unrelated to the concept of the divine sweetness is the notion that the characteristic of the kingdom of God, as enunciated by Jesus, is beatitude or happiness. When Jesus sketched the physiognomy of a life lived according to the new precepts of the kingdom, he spoke only in terms of a paradoxical happiness. Happy are those who are poor, who mourn, who weep, and who are persecuted. Why are they happy? Because somehow, beneath these exterior troubles, they have found something deeper that sustains and delights them. These adverse experiences, by detaching them from immediate gratifications, are making them more receptive to the delights that belong properly to the sphere of God. If it is true that "what is highly esteemed by human beings is an abomination before God" (Luke 16:15), then it must also be true that what is highly esteemed by God is an abomination to human beings. This is the contradiction inherent in the Gospel that reached its climax in the cross. The broad and easy road leads nowhere, but the "hard and rough road" ultimately leads to God and, even in the present life, we can say, "Your promises are sweeter to my taste than honey to my mouth" (Ps 118:103). It is the experience of this sweetness that sustains us in our journey.

20

Behold, in his kindness the Lord is showing us the road of life.

Just in case our attention is beginning to flag, Saint Benedict prods us to a sharper awareness by his admonitory "Behold." He is shaking us out of the sort of drowsiness that an excess of words can cause and telling us to open our eyes and look more closely. What is happening around us is that in the words of Scripture Christ ("the Lord") is pointing out to us the road by which we make progress toward a more complete life.

At the heart of this image of Christ as the one who points out the road, is the idea that without this guidance we are lost. If you have ever had the experience of being lost you will know that it is no fun. It is unpleasant to be in an unfamiliar part of a strange city where you cannot read the signs and you hesitate to ask directions because you do not know the local language. A great deal of energy is expended without ever coming closer to where you want to be; anxiety sets in, to be quickly followed by frustration and despair. The more clearly we know where we want to be, the more distressed we feel at not knowing how to get there. Any intelligible sign that sets us on the right road is very welcome and a cause of relief and joy. Likewise, those who have ever been lost in bushland know that there is a tendency to keep going around in circles without any sense of coming closer to where you should be.

Sometimes we tend to think that our journey to God is along a single road. Once we get onto that road, it is simply a matter of following it to the end. Human life is, however, far more complicated than that. And the spiritual journey itself necessarily leads beyond comfortable limits. Our course cannot be preprogrammed by a single, definitive choice made at the beginning and set to run the rest of our life by autopilot.

We have to keep making choices as each new situation presents itself. Because we are not always in top form spiritually, not all the choices we make are right. And so it is that we often find ourselves off the track and confused. Somehow we have to drag ourselves back on course. This is a fairly regular occurrence for most of us. Unthinkingly we drift off course and then we have to take steps to realign ourselves. Once or twice during life these deviations and detours are so serious that we find ourselves not only off course but completely lost and so upset that we are ready to abandon the journey. These periods of desperation can be life-or-death situations, but they may also be occasions for new conversions.

In the spiritual life the call to conversion manifests itself only at a particular moment, when various factors have made us vulnerable and ready for change. This critical juncture has been called "the tipping point," when a relatively minor matter can serve as a catalyst for major change—as it were, the straw that breaks the camel's back. There is energy in this call to conversion that makes it possible for us to take the step so long postponed and to set out more resolutely on the path that has opened up before us. The negative aspect of this phenomenon is that if the window of opportunity is ignored and the moment of grace is allowed to slip past us unheeded, it becomes ever so much more difficult to change direction later on. Instead of making the turn when we should have made it, we continue as we were and end up, at a later point in our life, having to backtrack in an effort to find the missed intersection. This detour can cost us many years.

Saint Benedict wants us to recognize that even now Christ is pointing out to us the way we should go. This is done not in a dictatorial way but as an act of kindness. We are lost and wandering, cast adrift in a boundless sea, and Christ, through his word echoing in our conscience, points out to us the way that leads not only back to the place from which we went astray but to a point further along and closer to our goal.

Jesus not only indicates the road to us, he is himself the road, the only road that leads to the fullness of truth and life. In practical terms, this means that we find guidance in his words and example that can help us get back on track so that we can resume our journey. But we need to remain attuned to his voice so that we can keep making whatever course alterations are necessary at each moment. A satellite navigation device serves no purpose unless it is switched on; so too we cannot expect to be guided by Christ unless we remain attentive to his word, both in the Scriptures and in the promptings of our conscience.

The directions we receive from Christ are the expression of love; they should be for us a source of deep consolation and happiness, knowing that, with such a guide, we will not easily go astray. Far from being angry or resentful at having to rely on outside guidance, we should be relaxed and grateful that someone else is taking care of navigating.

In this context it is worth returning to Psalm 118 (in the liturgical Psalter). The various terms referring to the manifestation of God's word—his law, his statutes, his commands—occur in nearly every verse of the psalm, and their impact on us is consistently described in positive terms. God's word is for us a lamp for our feet and a light for our path. Attending to it is a source of joy and delight. "Your promise is sweeter to my taste than honey in the mouth." Being schooled by God's law makes us grow in understanding and wisdom and protects us from being led astray by delusion and falsehood. "I am a traveler upon the earth; show me your commands. . . . I am like a lost sheep; seek your servant, for I have remembered your commands."

We do not have to feel lost because, in his kindness, the Lord is showing us the road to a fuller and more lasting life.

Therefore, with our loins girded with faith and the observance of good deeds, let us set out on his journeys with the guidance of the Gospel, so that we may be worthy to see the one who has called us into his kingdom.

In this verse Saint Benedict clearly enunciates the destination of all our traveling: we are on the road that leads to the heavenly kingdom, where we will be filled with the vision of God. Of course, the "kingdom of God" is not a place that can be found on a map. It is, rather, a desirable state of being as this was described by Jesus, beginning in this life and reaching its culmination in the next. No doubt this is why Saint Benedict speaks about "*his* journeys" rather than "*our* journeys."

The state of perfect discipleship is not the beginning of our traveling but its termination. We may have a lot of enthusiasm at the beginning, but enthusiasm alone does not make us perfect disciples; for that, a total conformity must exist between our will and God's will. And this is not achieved easily or quickly. And it is not simply a step that is taken once and for all. Throughout the long years of our life we will have many journeys to make: some major and others minor. And we will have to learn to tolerate the fact that our following of Christ is far from perfect; we are not yet what we would like to become. We are still on the road—making progress, it is to be hoped—but we have not yet arrived. There are still new journeys ahead of us. And, meanwhile, we remain our spotty selves.

The journeys that lead to Christ's kingdom are *his* journeys because they stem from his initiative, not ours. He has called us to enter his kingdom. We endure the hardships and dangers of traveling because the journey comes from

Christ's invitation and not from any spontaneous decision of our own. On a practical level, it is very important that we do not forget the fundamental experience of Christian or monastic vocation, or that Christ has said, "You did not choose me, I chose you" (John 15:16). There will be times in which the going will be hard or unexciting, and continuance will demand endurance. At times like this it will be a strong sense of personal vocation that will help us to keep moving.

We are never moving blindly: we have the Gospel as our guide. The Rule sees itself as no more than a practical compendium of Gospel living, albeit designed for the particular situation of a monastery. When we think about the guidance of the Gospel, our minds may go, first of all, to its moral precepts and its ethical ideals. These are certainly an integral part of the Gospel message, but they are only a part. The Gospel is fundamentally a proclamation of the Good News; it is something that excites, motivates, and encourages us. It is more than the dreary listing of a series of moral precepts. It is the promise of power that comes down from on high to give us the wisdom, understanding, and fortitude to put those impossible precepts into practice.

The promises of Christ conveyed to us in the Gospel provide entrance into the sphere of grace. They remind us that we are God's children and that we have been invited to address God by the intimate family name of *abba*. If it is true that our religious practice is effectively determined by the operative image we have of God, then, if we accept the Good News of God's fatherly love and affection for us, our religious response will be dominated by the ideal of reveling in the sunshine of God's love, of returning that love by prayer and thanksgiving, and by living in a manner that mirrors God's indulgent love for us. To be guided by the Gospel is to be liberated from the tyranny of law and superego and to allow our lives to be more and more marked by the simplicity of love. It does not mean extracting moral precepts from the words of Jesus and erecting them into a code or canon of behavior. It means living as Jesus lived by moving toward the fullness of self-giving love that he manifested during his time on earth.

We are not on our own as we travel along the road and engage in the onerous task of spiritual warfare. Christ who calls us is always with us. It is easy, however, for this truth to slip from our minds, unless we make an active effort to maintain our awareness. Christ is at the origin of our journey by calling us. Christ accompanies us on our way by his grace. Christ is our future and our final destination since our journey is directed toward that ultimate vision of God that is the fulfillment of all human aspirations.

For the moment we must be active on two fronts. We need to gird our loins, as Saint Benedict says, both by our faith in the unseen presence of Christ and by our practical willingness to engage in those good deeds by which faith is expressed and embodied. We notice again Saint Benedict's insistent yoking together of faith and good works and his reminder that we do ourselves no good by slackness or drifting, but we need to be vigorous in investing effort in the spiritual pursuit: "girding our loins" or, as we might say, rolling up our sleeves and getting down to work.

And let us not lose sight of where we are going or what will happen when we arrive. We are journeying toward the vision of God—the vision that is often termed "beatific" because it communicates to us the totality of human beatitude. The interior happiness the true disciple experiences on earth, described by Jesus in the Beatitudes, is merely the foretaste of the superabundant happiness that awaits us at the end of our journey: a happiness and fulfillment that will make even the most anguishing travail seem like a "slight and momentary affliction." We need to keep this outcome in view. The best means of ensuring our perseverance is Saint Benedict's recommendation in the fourth chapter: "To desire eternal life with the whole of our spiritual longing" (RB 4.46).

22

We cannot arrive at the tent of this kingdom in which we want to dwell, except by running there by means of good deeds.

In line with the fundamental purpose of the Prologue, Saint Benedict continues to remind us that actions speak more loudly than words. He would certainly endorse what Saint Aelred of Rievaulx would later say to his monks: "What I wish to insist on is that you cannot come to this point [of contemplation] through slackness or indolence, but only by labors, vigils, fasts, tears, and contrition of heart" (*Sermo* 34.29). We all desire a share in the eternal kingdom; we all desire to taste its firstfruits here below, but sometimes we allow ourselves to be seduced by the delusion that there is a way of achieving this that does not involve sustained effort on our part. We easily forget that a saint such as Thérèse of Lisieux who proclaimed, "My way is a way of love," was, all the while, assiduous in translating that love into the practical acts of self-denial that constituted her "little way."

As we have seen, Saint Benedict clearly recognizes the primacy of grace, but he just as clearly affirms the necessity of our corresponding with grace by running—not walking—toward God's kingdom by means of good actions. "We cannot arrive at the tent of this kingdom in which we want to dwell, except by running there by means of good deeds."

There have been periods in the past in which religion seems to have become totally identified with the practice of morality so that the good news of God's grace has been submerged amid the multiplication of moral norms. Today the situation is quite different. As Pope John Paul II frequently lamented, our age seems to have lost a sense of sin. Where moral relativism prevails, the significance of external actions is diminished and the sense that the Gospel demands of its followers a new way of acting and responding is correspondingly diminished. It is not enough to be swept off our feet by oceanic feelings of peace and well-being and a sense of communion with the cosmos. We need to allow spiritual experience to become incarnate in our way of looking at things and in how we live.

There is no greater source of scandal in the modern world than the discovery that those who have been proclaiming the excellence of spirituality have themselves been leading hugely immoral lives. Even our secular world expects of religious persons that they lead good lives. People are shocked when this appropriate expectation is found to be baseless. Certainly we can sympathize with human weakness however it is manifested, but it is hard to have anything but contempt for the hypocrisy that proclaims impossibly high ideals while failing to put into practice even the most common norms of human decency.

If we wish to embrace a spiritual life, we need to recognize first that there are necessary obligations that accompany this high aspiration. Second, we may perhaps need also to recognize the importance of safeguarding ourselves against a seductive voice that whispers, "These things don't matter; you are still a good person." This kind of dissociation is an example of what Jean-Paul Sartre termed "bad faith." We are turning a blind eye to our failure to embrace a necessary concomitant of spirituality: the gradual transformation of attitudes and behavior.

Most religious persons are not overt hypocrites. Sin does not express itself in their lives through heinous crimes. More often their resistance to God's grace is expressed through sins of omission. Think of the judgment scene in the twenty-fifth chapter of Saint Matthew's gospel. Those who are rejected are not damned for murder or adultery. Their sins were sins of omission. They did not do the good that they were capable of doing, for which they had an opportunity and the necessary resources.

And it was not deliberate sin, committed out of malice. They sinned because they did not understand the moral imperatives crying out to them from their own particular situation. They did not exert themselves to see Christ in the needy and so their failure to come to his assistance was culpable; they closed their hearts and closed their eyes and closed their hands.

Saint Benedict must have been aware of the fact that sins of omission are particularly rife in monasteries and wherever religious practice is routine. When one dedicates a considerable part of the day to religious observances one may be reluctant to look for opportunities to do more. We have only a quantum of energy, and when that is spent in daily obligations, it can happen that we think we have done enough. Instead of keeping our eyes peeled for occasions in which somehow Christ may be served in our neighbor, we pass by heedlessly on the other side of the road. Perhaps this is why Saint Benedict introduced some wild cards into the game—situations that cannot be preplanned, and demand spontaneous acts of generosity: hospitality to strangers whose arrival cannot be predicted or controlled (RB 53.16), care of the sick (RB 36), concern for the special needs of the very young and very old (RB 37).

Routine is very important in developing good habits, but it should never lead to a diminishment of alertness. In fact, as the years progress and good habits are established, a monk normally becomes ever more sharply aware of the potential for doing good in the ordinary events of everyday life. His level of awareness increases. He becomes more conscious and so more conscientious. It is true to say that the whole purpose of monastic discipline is to sharpen conscience—what the French term *conscientisation*. The scope of conscience is increased as is the intensity of its voice. Conscience supplements the dictates of the Rule by its own authority and reveals new areas in which good may be accomplished.

Monastic life is a school in which conscience is formed and invigorated. This occurs not only through solitary prayer and *lectio divina* but also through immersion in the communal way of life. A person who consents to participate fully in monastic activities, who is inspired by the good example of those more advanced in the way of virtue, whose attitudes are shaped by immersion in the liturgy, inevitably becomes more sensitive to the promptings of conscience and through conscience of the Holy Spirit.

Routine goodness can easily lead to complacency and judgmental attitudes; a well-formed conscience, on the other hand, is always indicating new paths of progress. Those who have thus committed their lives to this high obedience have a continual sense of being beginners—far from being pleased with the distance already traversed, they are conscious only of how far they have to travel to attain full openness to the grace of God and a continuous sense of God's proximity. More and more they recognize their reliance on God's mercy; their own history of virtue seems unremarkable. Indeed, as Saint Benedict indicates at the end of his chapter on humility, the higher the monk climbs on the ladder, the more aware he becomes of his own sinful state and of his need for the merciful intervention of God. Meanwhile, far from resting on his laurels, he is content to keep on running so that, by good deeds, he may be found worthy to enter God's kingdom and dwell in his tent.

23

Let us, however, ask the Lord with the prophet, and say to him: "Lord who will dwell in your tent? Who will find rest on your holy mountain?"

We have been talking about the necessity of running by good deeds; now we are opening up the theme of resting.

We are called both to run and to rest. It could be that the rest being referred to here is that eternal rest to which we all aspire, but I do not think so. The best way to run, if you intend to do so for a long time, is to run in a relaxed and restful manner. When the muscles are alternately used and rested they do not so easily succumb to fatigue. It is the same in the spiritual or monastic life. There is a time for vigorous exertion and a time for relaxation and rest. Far from being enemies, resting and running support and sustain each other. Especially in the early stages of the spiritual life, prudence often has to intervene to temper enthusiasm, lest by running too fast we get ahead of ourselves. When an army moves, its progress can only be at the speed of its slowest components; the supply chain cannot keep pace with the cavalry, and so the cavalry has to wait for the support units to arrive. The outcome of battles is often determined by logistics: without fuel, ammunition, and food, the momentum cannot be maintained. The cavalry may be more glamorous but, as Napoleon once remarked, an army marches on its stomach.

Spiritual progress is by way of integration. Too much enthusiasm for particular practices, especially those devised by oneself for oneself, can leave aspects of our total reality excluded. Yes, it is good that we practice self-denial and give time to prayer, but this is no excuse for ignoring appropriate care of our health, maintenance of relationships, the obligation of work, and the prudent allocation of time for recuperation from our efforts. Spirituality should never be allowed to become a tyranny, binding us ever more slavishly to particular practices. On the contrary, spiritual progress is habitually signaled by a growth in freedom, in a certain lightness of being, and in simple, uncomplicated happiness. Being adamant about particular practices is often a sign of scrupulosity or excessive attention to the superego and will, if unabated, lead to ruin.

How do we find rest in this life when the much-quoted text from the book of Job reminds us that the life of the human being here on earth is one long military campaign (Job 7:1)? It is true that trials and temptations are typical of human existence, but, as Saint Gregory the Great is at pains to insist, God always grants us breathing spaces, opportunities to catch our breath, as it were, before continuing the struggle.

We often attribute our inability to find rest to pressing external causes—our responsibilities, our work, the actions of others, and so forth. These are certainly contributing factors, but they are not the main source of our unrestedness. We fail to find rest mainly because our hearts are divided. Whether we admit it or not, we have allowed ourselves to engage in behavior that is inconsistent with the ideals we consciously uphold. Our will is not single but allows itself to be pulled in opposite directions so that we neither make progress nor find rest. We are not masters of our own household. There is a fifth column at work within us crippling our ability to deal with adversity in a way that is constructive and creative. This is the reason why external events have the power to disturb us. Gandhi is reputed to have said that the way to have peace in the world is to have peace in the heart. Those who live in a state of constant irritation need look no further for its cause than within their own unsettled hearts. The advice Saint Benedict gives to abbots applies to us all. We will never find rest if we are "turbulent or anxious, excessive or obstinate, overzealous or too suspicious" (RB 64.15). As he has already said, it is necessary for us actively to "seek after peace and pursue it." It is not enough to desire peace; we have to create peace. The way we begin to do this is by ensuring that our will is fixed on God, in whose will is peace. Then we try to ensure that our conduct is in effective harmony with the direction we have chosen.

In his chapter on humility Saint Benedict speaks about patience in terms of a silent consciousness. To endure external difficulties requires an interior silence that does not protest or make a great issue about even manifest injustice but absorbs the blows that life inflicts without becoming disoriented or vengeful. The Rule is perfectly clear about the fact that harsh and difficult things await the one who travels on the road that leads to God (RB 58.8). There is no need to be surprised when hard times come, but there needs to be growth in the skills of finding peace when everything goes wrong. Without such equanimity we will never find rest.

What are the qualities that enable us to remain constant when the going is rough? Four areas may be mentioned. We need to remain faithful to the way of life we have adopted, to be faithful to *lectio*, liturgy, personal prayer, and whatever else keeps us in contact with the spiritual world; these life-giving observances are a necessary part of any solution to difficulties. Second, we need to develop a wholesome respect for the workings of divine Providence that often manages to write straight on crooked lines: "It is good for me that I have been humbled so that I may learn your statutes" (Ps 118:71). The classic work by Jean-Pierre de Caussade, *On Abandonment to Divine Providence*, has helped many. Third, we need a certain robustness in our attitude to life, not ex-pecting that it will be "roses, roses all the way and never a trace of mud." We will be much more resilient and able to get back to normal more quickly if we get it into our heads that unless we can endure the rough and tumble of human life, we will get nowhere and may even drown in self-pity. Finally, and perhaps fundamentally, we need to have an es-chatological vision, recognizing that "if for this life only we have hope in Christ Jesus then of all people are we the most to be pitied" (1 Cor 15:19). Our spiritual journey is a journey that has not yet reached its destination: it is the ardent hope of arriving that keeps us moving. Without hope we will soon fall by the wayside.

Interior rest is possible only to the extent that we have acquired a substantial degree of self-knowledge. For this to happen we need space in our lives. A person who is always busy with something may perhaps be keeping occupied as a means of avoidance. So long as I am fussing about this urgency or that, I have a pretext for not dealing with matters that are important, even though they are less urgent. We need to have gaps in our activities, not only in order to reflect on our deeper concerns, but also to allow what is hidden below the threshold of consciousness to manifest itself. If we are really serious about spiritual life we will recognize the need for ample leisure in which issues may be allowed to surface and so be dealt with. So long as there are areas of our life that escape scrutiny, areas that are ignored, denied, rationalized, or repressed, we will never find rest.

A restful life derives from a balance of activities rather than from total inactivity. Just as in the house of God there is scope for both Mary and Martha, so too there is room for each of the sisters in our own lives—times of work and times of prayerful leisure; times of running and times of rest; times of working on self-improvement and times of delighting to see the working of grace, transforming our lives into something far more beautiful than we ourselves could ever imagine or achieve.

After this question, brothers, let us listen to the Lord answering, showing us the road to his tent.

The word "tent" appears in each of the last three verses. After speaking twice about dwelling in the Lord's tent, Saint Benedict now allows the question to arise concerning the road by which we travel to arrive there. It is a curious confusion of ideas. A tent is not a fixed abode but a portable shelter that we carry on a journey or erect on a temporary basis. The tent is not usually a destination at the end of a road.

Perhaps the reference to a tent in these verses has some special connotation. The best suggestion is that the psalm Saint Benedict is quoting is probably referring to the "tent of meeting," God's dwelling place among his people as they made their long journey through the wilderness to the Promised Land. This is the way this tent is described in the book of Exodus:

> Moses used to take a tent and pitch it outside the camp at a distance, and he called it the "tent of meeting." All who were seeking the LORD would go to the tent of meeting, which was outside the camp. Whenever Moses went out to the tent, all the people rose and stood at the entrances to their own tents, watching Moses until he entered the tent. And it happened that when Moses entered the tent, the pillar of cloud would descend and stand at the entrance, while the LORD spoke with Moses. When all the people saw the pillar of cloud standing at the entrance to the tent, they all stood up and bowed down, each at the entrance to his tent. The LORD used to speak to Moses face to face, as a man speaks with his friend. (Exod 33:7-11)

This is a very profound passage that provides an interesting background to what Saint Benedict is thinking. The tent to which the monk desires to have access is the place where he will encounter the Lord. He has come to the monastery seeking God, and he makes progress along the monastic road only in so far as he continues to seek. When the search is less intense, he slows down. If he stops seeking then he begins to go off the track and soon, if he does not return, he will become confused and disoriented. The search for God is the origin and purpose of the monastic journey.

The text says that all who seek God must go to the tent of meeting, which was outside the camp. It is all very well to say that we seek God in all our routine everyday activities, even though our attention is fully focused on whatever it is that we are doing. But to encounter God deeply we need to take time out, to go apart from the camp, and to seek the place where it is possible to speak with the Lord face-to-face, giving God our full attention.

We are not always clear enough on the mystical component of Benedictine spirituality. It is easy to forget that its whole purpose is to provide us with a map that will lead us to the tent of meeting, to a profound and intimate encounter with God. Let us not forget that the whole reason for our spiritual or monastic journey is that we may meet up with God. When prayer, in its various forms, occupies a substantial part of our day, whatever difficulties we may encounter are seen in perspective. If, however, we allow prayer to slip out of our lives, then hard times will tend to impact us heavily. It is hard to maintain our equanimity when our spiritual life is not being nourished by contact with God.

The subtle experience of God's presence is both profoundly satisfying and profoundly unsatisfying. It is satisfying because it corresponds to the most intimate aspiration of our being and the purpose of our choosing to follow the monastic or spiritual path. Paradoxically, it is simultaneously unsatisfying because the more intense our experience, the stronger our desire to penetrate more fully into the divine mystery. We realize that what we have touched is but the outer edge of God's garment and we are drawn to desire more.

The book of Exodus describes Moses in a similar quandary. "Show me your Glory," he says to the Lord in ardor of spirit. But God replies, "You cannot see my face and go on living." Even Moses, the friend of God, hidden in a cleft of the rock, saw only God's back as he moved past him (Exod 33:18-23). The experience of God here on earth does not fully satisfy us or extinguish our desire; rather, it makes our longing to be close to God all the more intense. As Saint Bernard says, rather than throwing water on the fire to extinguish it, contact with God is more like throwing oil on the flames of our desire; far from quenching them, it makes them burn more fiercely.

Another more imaginative way of looking at "the tent" recalls the well-known verse in the Prologue of the Fourth Gospel: "The Word became flesh and pitched his tent among us" (John 1:14). In the new dispensation, God's tent of meeting is the humanity of the Word become flesh. Here is where we encounter God, in "the man Christ Jesus, the mediator between God and humankind" (1 Tim 2:5). And if we want to know the road to the tent, the answer is simple. Jesus himself said, "I am the road" (John 14:8).

The mysticism of the Benedictine tradition is Christocentric. This is clear not only from the Rule itself but also from the titles of the books written by Dom Columba Marmion: *Christ the Life of the Soul, Christ in his Mysteries, Christ the Ideal of the Priest, Christ the Ideal of the Monk.* To become spiritual it is first necessary to becomes fully human, to accept our own humanity in all its ambiguity. And the best way to be reconciled with our own humanity is by seeing this same humanity brought to its perfect fulfillment in Christ. The reason why Saint Benedict's approach to life is often called "humane" and why the Benedictine tradition is famous for its humanity is simply that both find their supreme model in Christ.

To find rest in God's tent is to feed our soul by engineering into our lives many opportunities for encountering God in Christ. It means that in times of joy, as in times of sadness, we are familiar with the pathways that lead us to the tent of meeting.

He says: "The one who enters without stain and practices righteousness."

Throughout Western mystical tradition there has been a strong ethical stream. Although an intense experience of God can erupt at any time—for example, as a stimulus on the road to conversion—the slow build up of an abiding sense of familiarity with God usually presupposes a fairly consistent effort to lead a good life. "It is not enough to live entirely for Christ," says Saint Bernard, "one must have done it for a long time." Saint Benedict is using the words of the psalm to convey this message: if you want to make your way toward the encounter with God, then first of all lead a moral life. It all comes back to the verse that was used earlier in the Prologue, "Turn away from evil and do good."

The image the psalmist uses is of being "without stain," undefiled, clean, pure, free from filth. This image belongs to one of three symbolic families used to convey the effect that sin has on our conscience. To the extent that we are under the power of sin, our conscience feels stained or defiled, it feels lost or off the track, or it feels oppressed by a deadening sense of heaviness, an acquired helplessness to do good. Sin is a stain, a going astray, a psychological weight. These are the principal similitudes employed in the Bible to describe the effect of resistance to God's grace: uncleanness, confusion, lack of freedom. In this way it is our inner experience that attests to the damage inflicted on us by sin. These are not punishments inflicted by God or by external agents. They are the automatic residue of behavior that is contrary to the noblest tendencies of human nature. When we sin we defile ourselves, we lose our mental integrity, and we submit to a powerlessness to act as we should. We are the creators of our own misery.

The anthropology underlying these images is that our humanity is diminished by rebellion against God. God is not harmed by our sin; we hurt ourselves. This, surely, is the whole thrust of the story of the first fall recounted in the book of Genesis. An idyllic existence is transformed into something "solitary, poor, nasty, brutish and short," as Thomas Hobbes wrote in *Leviathan* (I.13). This is the biblical answer to the question of human suffering: in turning away from God we turn away from the possibility of human happiness and fulfillment. The whole purpose of monastic life is to reverse this process: "by the labor of obedience, you will return to him from whom you have withdrawn by the slackness of disobedience."

The one who approaches God without stain is the one whose conscience is clear. This interior clarity is in marked contrast to the muddiness and turmoil of those who admit moral compromises into their life. We are purified by our obedience to the truth (1 Pet 1:22). When we turn away from the truth, hide from the truth, or distort its meaning, we lose this inner transparency. If the conscience is clouded, the inner self is alienated from God and sinks deeper into stagnation. On the other hand, when the conscience is clear, the radiance of God easily penetrates through the self to the inner core of our being and begins or continues the work of transformation.

In more recent times, the idea of purity is often associated with freedom from sexual sin. In the monastic tradition, the concept of purity, as in "purity of heart," is much broader. It signifies a basic disposition of a will that is undivided, consistent, harmonious. And while it is true that sexuality is an area in which inconsistencies easily arise, the real problem is more often deeper than lust. It is the failure of the will to fix itself upon a single objective. Where such simplicity of purpose is lacking the person falls under the influence of whatever wind blows from whatever direction. As we read in the Epistle of

James (Jas 1:6-8), "The one who wavers is like a wave of the sea, blown about and tossed by the wind. Let such a person not think to receive anything from the Lord. The person in two minds is unstable in everything that is done." Sexual sin, like every other sin, is the result of a divided heart, a double mind, a will that cannot decide whether to be good or not.

This is why the reality underlying Saint Benedict's insistence on stability in commitment is stability of mind and heart—the will fixed enduringly on a single objective. To the extent that this ideal is realized, the person will experience a deep sense of interior peace that is able to survive the severest external challenges to its serenity. A heart free from stain is a pure heart, an undivided heart, a stable heart, a heart that easily slides into prayer when outward duties cease to occupy its attention.

To enter without stain is to be like the church that is called to be "without stain or wrinkle or any other blemish, but holy and blameless" (Eph 5:26). No doubt Saint Benedict would have made his own the admonition of the Second Epistle of Peter: "Make every effort to be found spotless, blameless, and at peace with God" (2 Pet 3:13). What else can be asked of any Christian?

26

"The one who speaks truth in the heart and does not commit deceit with the tongue."

A characteristic quality of one who is taking seriously the search for God is a substantial harmony between what is on the inside and what is apparent externally. What you see is what you get! The practice of righteousness is important, but it is of value only if it stems from a righteous heart, and is the expression of an interior disposition. It is from the heart that the moral quality of all action flows.

If we take for granted that those for whom the Rule was written will be engaged in all sorts of good works, then "to speak truth in the heart" must be taken to mean, in part, avoiding the tendency to engage in discordant internal dialogue while all the while performing appropriately virtuous actions. There are many ways in which the heart, mind, and imagination can be singing a different song from exterior behavior; the greatest treason of all is to practice virtue for unworthy motives. Included among these ways is what Saint Benedict will later describe as "murmuring": doing what we are supposed to but with subversive intent, all the while grumbling and complaining interiorly. Benedict, as is well known, is unusually severe in this matter. This is what he says: "And if the disciple obeys with an evil disposition and murmurs, not only by mouth but even in the heart, even though he obeys the order, it will not be acceptable to God who looks upon the heart of the one who murmurs. For this he will earn no grace but will incur the penalty of those who murmur—if he does not amend and make satisfaction" (RB 5.17-19). Murmuring signals that what is done externally is done under constraint; such doers of good actions do so because they are compelled. Their virtuous deeds are not expressive of interior disposition. There is a fundamental discord between what is seen and what takes place within their hearts.

The sign of a truly upright person is a concordance among thought, word, and action. If there is untruth in the heart or deceit on the tongue, external virtue is of little value. In fact, good behavior can easily serve either as compensation or as a disguise for a heart given over to vice. Jesus recognized this reality and it was for this disharmony that he rebuked the professional religious people of his time: "Woe to you, teachers of the Law and you Pharisees. Hypocrites! You are like whitewashed sepulchers, which look beautiful on the outside but inside are full of the bones of the dead and all that is unclean. So, on the outside you appear to people as righteous, but inside you are full of hypocrisy and wickedness" (Matt 23:27-28). This is, in a sense, a problem that many good people experience and one that Benedict warns against later in the Rule: "Do not wish to be called holy before being so, but first be holy so that it may be more truthfully said" (RB 4.62).

Here again it is worth underlining the importance of effective self-knowledge. There are three advantages that flow from realistic self-assessment: we are protected from delusions of grandeur, we are less inclined to be harsh in judging others, and we lay the foundations for the development of a compassionate stance toward other people. Knowing ourselves well means that we are less inclined to take liberties with the truth on the grounds that we are superior to the rest of humanity, believing that the usual norms do not apply to us—that we are the exceptions to the rule. We are human, as the ancient poet wrote, and nothing that is human is foreign to us—including human imperfection.

It is important for us to be aware of what is going on in our imaginations, with a view to assessing the value of our fantasies and taking steps to ensure that they do not subtly undermine what we are consciously trying to achieve in our lives. Using the words of the psalm, Saint Benedict proposes to his followers that the pursuit of contemplative experience must be accompanied by an equal pursuit of a basic integrity that includes our thoughts and our speaking. This, of course, is much easier said than done. There is a certain wild and unpredictable element in our thoughts that resists control and constantly veers away from the direction we wish to give to our lives. All who give themselves to good living are afflicted with contrary imaginations that are simultaneously distressing and attractive. And our speech often takes its cue from these secret imaginings.

The fantasies that occupy us in moments when nothing else is going through our heads, such as in the period before we fall asleep, can be important diagnostic agents in assessing the quality of our subjective dispositions. What are we really like when we stop trying to be good? What sort of person underlies our efforts to conform to an acceptable standard of behavior? It is because we are often unaware of what sort of persons we really are that we are sometimes surprised by the venom that infects our speech or the subtle malice that can permeate our behavior. Only good can come from paying attention to what rises spontaneously in our thoughts.

In the seventh chapter of Saint Mark's Gospel, Jesus lists all the awful things that have their residence in the human heart: evil thoughts, sexual immorality, theft, murder, adultery, greed, malice, deceit, lewdness, envy, slander, arrogance, and stupidity (Mark 7:21-22). If you do not recognize yourself in this list, then probably your self-knowledge is defective. Righteousness is measured not only by the probity of our actions but also by the quality of our unguarded thoughts. It is only when our hearts are purified by the enduring action of the Holy Spirit that we attain that transparency of being that enables us sometimes to enter into the full contemplative experience of God.

And how do we know that we have reached this degree of purity of heart? It is surely when our thoughts no longer dissent from the basic purpose of our life and our tongues refrain from all manner of deceit. This means more than literal truthfulness. It signifies that we have renounced the manipulative use of language to further our own prospects, the truth that lacks compassion, the shaded meaning that impugns another's integrity. As we read in the Epistle of James, "Those who never sin with their tongues are already perfect" (Jas 3:2).

Saint Benedict is uncompromising: if we want to meet God, then we must speak truth in our heart and not commit deceit with our tongue. He is so insistent on this necessity that, in chapter 4, he returns to the theme, admonishing the monk "to bring forth truth from the heart and the mouth" (RB 4.28). He has truly made his own the lesson conveyed by the psalm.

"The one who does no evil to a neighbor or allows dishonor against a neighbor."

Saint Benedict continues to follow the text of the psalm in speaking about the conditions to be fulfilled if we are to find rest on God's holy mountain; we are to do no evil to our neighbor, and we are not to become agents or accomplices in a neighbor's disgrace.

First of all, we might note that it is about our treatment of our neighbors that Saint Benedict is speaking. It is easy enough to feel a vaguely universal benevolence toward humanity in general—the more distant the better! We demonstrate the seriousness of our commitment to following the way of Christ not by such fluffy sentiments but by the enduring effort to treat well those who are closest to us—those most likely to have plans different from ours or to infringe on our treasured autonomy. We may cherish the fondest feelings for the people of Greenland, but these are bootless unless we happen to live in that country. Our love and compassion are measured by the way we deal with our immediate neighbors. As they say, "Charity begins at home."

So, how do we treat those closest to us? As with the Hippocratic oath, the basic ethical demand is that we do no harm to others. Most of us, because we are good people, could probably draw up a long list of the bad things we have not done to those around us. But is this enough? If it is true that the daily sins of good people are mostly sins of omission, is it enough to avoid doing wrong to our neighbors? Don't we also have a complementary obligation to do good? If omission stems from unawareness, then don't we have also the obligation to make ourselves aware of the needs of others with a view to meeting some of them? We have actively to search out those that need help instead of waiting to trip over them.

The law of charity is all-encompassing; we sin against our neighbors by failing to love them. We don't have to do positive wrong to them or to give vent to malice against them. By failing to love them affectively and effectively we are doing our neighbor an injustice. The opposite of love is not red-hot hatred: it is coldness, coolness, indifference. It is a willful refusal to be touched by another's plight, a failure to rejoice with those who rejoice and to mourn with those who mourn. We see ourselves as islands of righteousness, unconnected to others, receiving nothing from them and owing them nothing in return. Such a stance is effectively to deny or restrict the social element in human nature, and to turn our back on the truth that we are all members of Christ's body.

Saint Aelred of Rievaulx has a distinctive view of one of love's greatest enemies. He thinks that this is envy. This makes us look upon our neighbors with a jaundiced eye, rejoicing in their misfortune and being saddened by their success. Such contrariness not only is unfair to others, but also has an insidiously destructive effect on ourselves. Saint Aelred writes, "Believe me, my brothers, there is nothing that so diminishes the joys of this present life or removes the hope of future happiness or simultaneously undermines all the other virtues [as envy]" (*Sermo* 55.6). Envy does not manifest itself openly; it is usually disguised, presenting itself as reasonable criticism, as merely trying to bring somebody down to their proper size.

A failure to value the talents of others, to appreciate their worth and to praise them when they have done well is an injustice, whatever rationalizations we may offer as an excuse.

Worse than merely allowing the goodness of others to be unaffirmed and without due honor is to become a party to their disgrace. The Latin text of the psalm used by the Master and Benedict is difficult to translate, as is the Hebrew original. Literally, it speaks of one "who does not accept opprobrium against a neighbor." The object of this prohibition can be taken either actively or passively: it can signify either active efforts to bring a neighbor to disgrace or merely allowing ourselves to become complicit in their shame. In the latter sense Terrence Kardong gives it the meaning of listening to slander against a neighbor. However we solve this puzzle, it is not entirely sure whether Benedict or the Master were doing more than using the verse of the psalm in a general sense: to be worthy to climb God's mountain we must avoid any behavior that contributes to a neighbor's dishonor.

In chapter 4, verse 8, Saint Benedict instructs his disciples to honor every human being; in a certain sense, the community that he envisaged was one in which mutual honor and respect was an important component. To honor others is to avoid being complicit in any situation in which they might be shamed. This was especially important in the sort of culture familiar to Saint Benedict, where any diminishment of social acceptance would have been experienced as undermining a sense of identity, a loss of face. This dependence on the approval of others is one of the reasons why excommunication would have been considered such a terrible punishment. To be cut off from the primary network of social support would have condemned the individual to a very uncomfortable and unaccustomed solitariness. In chapter 70 Saint Benedict insists that nobody, apart from the abbot, may inflict such a serious penalty; in fact, he makes provision for pastoral intervention that does not involve publication of what has been done (RB 46.5-6) but, instead, acts in secret to mitigate the sense of hopelessness that unavoidable isolation brings (RB 23.2; 27.3).

Shame is one of the most potent forms of punishment; the person shamed is declared thereby to be unworthy of honor. Shame is used in the family, at school, and in society at large to enforce current norms by dishonoring those who do not conform to them. Our judicial system uses shame extensively. It is a disgrace to be hauled up before a magistrate, and the architecture of the courtroom leaves little doubt about the inferiority of the person indicted vis-à-vis the majesty of the court.

When we judge another's conduct harshly, whether we use real or imagined grievances as our starting point, we often make the leap from disapprobation of the behavior to a dismissal of the person. We use shame as a means to make a person feel bad not only about what they have done but about themselves. We publish their misdoings so that the other person drowns in a sea of rejection. We, the righteous, band together to say to the perceived sinner, "You are not one of us." Shame inflicted on others is like an excommunication; it banishes offenders from the company of their peers and condemns them to bruising solitude.

Shaming is an ineffectual means of correction. It may seem like a rapid solution to inappropriate behavior, but more often than not it generates a huge tide of resentment whose eddies continue for decades. Monks and nuns often exhibit elephantine powers of recall, and it takes very little prompting for long-cherished grievances to come to the surface. Events of thirty or forty years ago continue to feed their sense of being treated unfairly. Far from being a stimulus to a better life, the hurtful shame occasioned by a particular experience makes them more intransigent, defending their behavior and fashioning a whole system of values to support it.

Much better than shaming is to reinforce persons' sense of self-worth and to give them space to reframe their lives according to more wholesome values. Formation of conscience is the only permanent basis for a good life; trying to live so as to gain the approval of others is ultimately futile. Therefore, we do no good to others by making them feel ashamed of themselves. Whatever passing benefit we may hope for, there is a strong possibility that our attitudes and actions will cause ongoing harm. Jesus seems to have preferred the company of those whom the self-righteous rejected as "sinners." We who are his disciples have to recognize that we will catch more flies with a spoonful of honey than with a bucketful of vinegar and that any effort to help people by making them feel bad about themselves will be ultimately self-defeating. We may not allow ourselves to become the agents or accomplices in another's shame.

28

"One who rejects and annihilates the malign devil when he suggests something, [driving him] out of sight of the heart; one who grabs the thoughts born of him and beats them against [the rock that is] Christ."

The devil is mentioned only four times in the Rule. Apart from the present instance, the devil is seen as the principal adversary against whom the monk contends in 1.4, as the one who takes advantage of a monk's disappointment to lead him into greater difficulties (RB 54.4), and as the one who persuades the professed monk to quit the monastery (RB 58.28).

Taken together, these four texts suggest that Saint Benedict sees diabolic influence at work whenever a monk is exposed to temptations, particularly fundamental temptations

that undermine the stability of his vocation. We need to remember, however, that Saint Benedict is operating less out of
a mythic mind-set with a developed demonology than from
the common experience of those who are serious about their
commitment to a monastic or spiritual life. The more strongly
one is committed to living a good life, the more insistently
one is assailed by contrary imaginations. These may take the
form of being attracted to the kinds of activities that one
has so recently renounced or, on the other hand, being overcome by weariness and discouragement at the thought of how
much more needs to be done. The vigor of the temptation is
proportionate to the seriousness of one's commitment. The
absence of temptation or the appearance of only the mild-
est of temptations may indicate that one's following of the
spiritual path is already lukewarm and unlikely to endure.
Because such suggestions seem independent of the person's
fundamental orientation and even contrary to the will, they
were ascribed to external agents, that is, they were thought
to derive from diabolic temptation. We perhaps may think of
them as coming more often from our own private fund of repressed fantasies and instinctual tendencies. These sometimes
reassert themselves when the mind is relatively disengaged
to surprise us, perhaps, with attractions that seem to go in a
direction opposite to what we have freely chosen; reminding
us that spiritual warfare is far more elemental than the facile
exercise of willpower.

All temptation begins at the level of thought. The imagination is porous and we do not have absolute control over
the thoughts, desires, attractions, and fantasies that find entrance there, no more than we can exercise control over the
content of our dreams. As a result, no matter how strong our
mental discipline, we cannot prevent wild and unwholesome
thoughts appearing on the surface of our minds. At the level
of thought, each one of us is capable of the most heinous
crimes. In the monastic perspective all the various vices are

innate, resident in a hidden zone of the heart, waiting for an opportunity to come forth and lead us astray. Errant thoughts were considered to be the offspring of these inherent vices, the first stage in translating tendencies into actions.

Great importance was attached to recognizing these thoughts and ensuring that they do not begin to find a permanent resting place in consciousness from where they could begin to grow to the point where they can influence our behavior. The thought is the parent of the act. Let me give a concrete example. I see another person chuckling, and the thought comes to my mind that I am the object of this mirth. Quickly the thought joins to itself the resentments I have accumulated over the years about being mocked. Now the thought is being transformed into a feeling. Perhaps other similar instances, real or imagined, cause the resentment to turn into anger, and very soon it is going to be translated into action—by a violent outburst, by subtle calumny, by passive aggression, by the withholding of affection, or by some other way of making the other person feel a pain proportionate to the pain I felt when I imagined that I was being laughed at. All very understandable, but look at the origins of the whole process. Another's involuntary action is interpreted negatively by me—with very little objective evidence. The thought becomes a feeling; the feeling builds up a head of steam and soon becomes a hostile action. And all the while I am unaware that my response is disproportionate to the event that triggered it. The thought is but a droplet that falls into the mind, but once it grows powerful it can sweep me away like a river in spate.

If I had somehow interrupted this sequence, I would not have attacked the other person. If had slowed down the onrush of feeling and submitted the thought to scrutiny, my peace and contentment would have been undisturbed. Where does this thought come from? Is there another explanation? To what sort of action does it lead? Does the behavior to which I am being drawn really express the sort of person I wish to be? Speed is the enemy. If I have the sense to slow down the process and examine the elements of the situation, I am more likely to make a choice of action that is more consonant with my fundamental priorities.

The trick consists in recognizing these incipient thoughts for what they are: expressions of the shadow side of my nature and the first steps on the road to self-destruction. We cannot stop them impinging on our awareness, but we can take steps to prevent their nesting there. Often it is not so much a matter of chasing the thoughts away, attempting to brush them off as if they were flies. Because these thoughts link up with realities deep inside us, they are not easily flicked away; like flies we chase away, they simply come back from a different direction. Saint Benedict wants us to take these troublesome thoughts to prayer, using the imagery of Psalm 136, to dash them against the rock that is Christ. Instead of being passive before this subtly seductive train of thought, we should attempt to counterbalance it by setting it alongside the fundamental values we have chosen: our relationship with Christ, our commitment to a Gospel way of life, our search for God. How does this intrusive line of thought match up with my basic philosophy of life and the behavior that follows from it?

Public figures have to do this all the time; their integrity is doubted if they do not practice what they preach. A politician who constantly proclaims "family values" loses all credibility if serial adultery is made public. So every action must be scrutinized to see that it conforms to the image by which they market themselves. Nowadays, if a major political figure wants to smoke, he has to do it in the strictest privacy so as not to upset the antismoking lobby; he has to pretend to be enthusiastic about a sport in which he has no interest to please those who follow that sport. Everything has to be done to enhance the image most likely to be acceptable to most voters.

In our case it is less a matter of public reputation, since thoughts are invisible. We should, however, constantly ask ourselves whether what we allow to pass through our mind is consistent with what we deeply believe and cherish. A single thought probably does little damage. The erosion of our commitments happens gradually, sometimes over the course of years. A thought becomes a conviction that then assumes elements of desire; desire seizes an opportunity to become reality, and then it establishes a foothold in our behavior. We excuse ourselves and rationalize our behavior and meanwhile we develop a habitual manner of acting that is quite contrary to our most fundamental convictions. We tell ourselves that it is a matter of small importance, unaware that we ourselves are gradually being deflected from our goal and putting ourselves in a situation that will bring us nothing but frustration and unhappiness. And it all began with a thought.

Saint Benedict's suggestion about dashing the thought against the rock of Christ is repeated in his chapter On the Implements of Good Works. There he adds a corollary: "Immediately to dash the evil thoughts that come to one's heart on Christ and to make them known to a spiritual senior" (RB 4.50). This is an excellent but not the only way of bringing these nebulous thoughts into full consciousness. Having a conversation about thoughts and fantasies often makes it easier for us to perceive their unreality. It is also a means of profiting from the wisdom and discernment of an elder who has learned the art of discernment by doing battle with his own thoughts and has developed the skill of being able to recognize their origin and nature.

Thoughts are the least substantial part of human existence, yet they are important. Treating thoughts seriously is the only way to neutralize the subconscious resistances to our monastic and spiritual journey. To the extent that this inherent resistance is diminished, our will becomes single;

we are beginning to move toward that purity of heart that is next door to the vision of God.

29

Those who fear the Lord are not elated by their good observance, but consider that the good things in them cannot have come about from themselves but are from the Lord.

One of the traps in trying to be good is that to the extent that one is successful, there is a tendency to be pleased with oneself and self-congratulatory. "Because of my great efforts," we say, "I have overcome this tendency or developed this good habit." This is a natural enough response, just as it is natural to be disappointed when one fails to maintain a standard one has set for oneself. When we act the Good Samaritan and come to the aid of one needing assistance, we feel good about having done so and about ourselves. This inward self-approval is, in a sense, our reward for doing good.

There is a danger here. It is easy to put so much emphasis on our own efforts that we attribute the good that we do wholly to ourselves and implicitly conclude that our good actions indicate that everything is going well in our spiritual life. That may be a fair conclusion, but it can easily lull us into the kind of inattentiveness that Saint Benedict wishes us to avoid. "Vigilance is the price of freedom." As soon as we let down our guard we leave ourselves liable to temptation—and we can never be certain of a successful outcome. This is why we pray, "Lead us not into temptation."

The medieval monks used to say that a good conscience is a paradise. No exterior benefit can be fully enjoyed while a troubled conscience is gnawing within. And the life of virtue and goodness is certainly a source of great inward peace. It is prudent to remember, however, that even in that original paradise there was a serpent, and the serpent brought temptation, and temptation led to a fall.

If I were the devil, the way I would choose to tempt good people would be to lead them up the garden path of self-approval. I would suspend serious temptation for a while and make it easy for them to perform all sorts of visible good deeds so that they felt secure in their virtue and in the approbation of others. Perhaps I would encourage them to push themselves into even greater exertion than prudence would allow. Then, when they were tired or burned out I would strike a single deft blow and fell them in an instant. I would follow up with whispers that would cause shame and self-disgust and thus try to lead them into the abyss of despair from which it is very difficult to escape. This is where my strategy of temptation would finally lead, but it would begin with delusional self-approval, with their being elated by their good observance so that they lose all sense of dependence on God.

We have to work so hard at being good that sometimes we forget that the good we do is God working through us: inspiring the thought, revealing the means, giving us the energy, guiding us in its application, and helping us to keep on the job until the task is complete. When we do anything good, God's grace is operative within us to a greater extent than we easily perceive. Saint Benedict wants us to become ever more conscious of this as we go through our daily tasks. This is why, earlier in the Prologue, he instructs us to begin every good work prayerfully: "First, whenever you begin to do some good deed, ask [Christ] with most insistent prayer that he bring it to completion" (RB Prol. 4).

The other thing that can happen when we are busy congratulating ourselves for our performance is that we overlook the contributions that others have made—not only those who have formed in us the appropriate beliefs and values from which good actions spring, but also those who have provided us with the opportunity to do good. Without the neediness of others, our willingness to help would have been unfulfilled. As one who speaks, it has often been my experience that the best material is drawn out of me by the eagerness of the audience. I am inspired and energized by my hearers to go beyond my natural limits. The result is as much theirs as mine. When good things happen it is rare that a single person is responsible. Our best work is reliant on others in ways that we do not always realize.

When our self-esteem is built on the manifest goodness of our actions, we can easily become dependent on the approval of others, so that our strongest motivation for doing something becomes our search for praise and approbation. This approach is like the behaviorism we use to train children: a matter of reward and punishment. It is not appropriate for adults, for whom doing the right thing sometimes demands going against the prevailing opinion of right and wrong and standing firm on the basis of a well-formed conscience.

Again we are reminded of the importance of developing a well-formed conscience so that we are able to assess moral options in the light of truth—the truth of revelation, the truth of spiritual wisdom, the truth of our own nature and history. The self-knowledge that comes from living in the context of a true conscience enables us to have a sober sense of self-esteem that is not in thrall to excessive self-congratulation.

How do we ensure that our conscience is well formed? The means to use are readily available: regular contact with the Scriptures through *lectio divina*, being at pains to inform ourselves of the teaching of the church, allowing our beliefs and values to be profoundly shaped by our attachment to a community of faith, contact with a spiritual guide or mentor or supervisor who can help us unmask the operation of hidden motivations, and, sometimes, listening to those who are critical of us. Keeping our ears open to these various sources of guidance is a good guarantee that we will not go astray and a reasonable insurance against becoming deluded with false ideas about the state of our spiritual progress.

All of this is summed up pithily in one of Saint Benedict's implements of good work: "Not to want to be called holy before one is, but first to be holy so that it may more truthfully be said" (RB 4.62).

And so they magnify the Lord working in them, saying with the prophet: "Not to us, Lord, not to us, but to your name give the glory."

In the Old Testament, the outshining of God's presence in the world was termed "the glory of the Lord." God was made manifest among us through wonderful works of power and goodness: creation, redemption, revelation. The glory of God was something that, by its very nature, was out of this world yet was, by God's mercy, brought to earth to serve as a beacon for humanity, showing forth the path that leads to eternal life. Just as the hiding of God's face was seen as the ultimate calamity for humankind, so the manifestation of the divine glory was understood as our ultimate felicity.

The whole history of salvation can be viewed as the progressive self-revelation of a loving God: "And the glory of God will dwell in our land" (Ps 84:9). This revelation reaches its culmination in Christ, as Saint John says: "We have seen his glory, full of grace and truth" (John 1:14). All this belongs to the mystery of God's loving plan for us, but there is a hidden danger here. The divine glory is something proper to God and may not be claimed by any mortal being. The prophet Isaiah declares this in the name of God: "I am the LORD; that is my name! I will not give my glory to another or my praise to idols" (Isa 42:8). And, "For my own sake, for my own sake, I do this. How can I let myself be defamed? I will not yield my glory to another" (Isa 48:11). The ultimate arrogance of the human being is to appropriate God's glory, to take false credit for the works of God's mercy.

God's glory, God's holiness, is among us; it adheres to every aspect of human existence, giving a sacredness to everything in creation. It remains, however, God's glory. It cannot be claimed by any human agency. When we begin to use words like "glory" or "holiness" or "sacredness" of human beings and human institutions we debase the word itself. To God alone belongs glory. To God alone belongs holiness. Whatever we perceive of these qualities in people or even in ourselves is present only by God's gift and not because of any human prerogative or achievement.

Saint Benedict says that the correct response to our perception of some good in ourselves is to magnify the Lord. This is the only time in the whole Rule that the verb *magnificare* is used. The use of the phrase "magnify the Lord" must almost certainly be derived from the *Magnificat*, sung daily at Vespers (RB 17.8). Even though it is oblique, this is probably the only reference to the Mother of Lord in Benedict's Rule. When the monk becomes conscious of the victory of grace within him, Saint Benedict wants him to cry aloud in jubilation: "My soul magnifies the Lord; my spirit rejoices in God my Savior. . . . For the Almighty has done great things for me: Holy is God's name." There is no sense of self-congratulation here, only a profound awareness that God has looked with favor on the humility of his servant. This fundamental attitude of humility, so amply discussed in chapter 7 of the Rule, is the dominant spiritual attitude that Benedict hopes will flourish among his disciples. Humility is not a matter of putting oneself down or denying one's gifts and achievements, such as they are. It is an enduring spirit of gratitude and praise to God "for all that God has been pleased to manifest in his worker . . . by the action of the Holy Spirit" (RB 7.70).

The anticipated outcome of monastic life, or of any investment in spiritual living, is growth in goodness. There does not seem to be much point in expending so much effort if nothing results. And, unless we are particularly stupid, we will be conscious that progress has been made. Not immediately, of course, or definitively, but with time we will notice that what seemed difficult for us previously is becoming less arduous, sometimes easy, and occasionally even delightful. Yes, we do advance. The point that Saint Benedict is making is that he wants us to ascribe our progress not to our own puny efforts but to God working in us.

Aelred of Rievaulx was astute enough to notice that one of the more subtle temptations to which spiritual people are prey is the proneness to vainglory. This has two parts. The first tendency is to become excessively pleased with oneself and so drift into a dangerous complacency. The second is to become dependent on the approval, praise, and adulation of others so that conscience is disabled and there is a reluctance to invest in any course of good action that does not yield a harvest of applause. We are no longer free agents acting out of the highest motives; we are driven by human acclaim in much the same way as politicians who change their principles in accordance with the latest opinion polls.

This is what Aelred says in one of his talks to his monks:

> When virtue grows, humility is to be maintained. If vanity burdens, you know what a struggle it is for the mind that progresses to maintain its course. Love of human praise and flattery can cause the loss of discipline and the [prideful] swelling of the heart. The more the saints advance the more they

are wearied by the burden of vanity. In this way [the more] they lift themselves up to higher things [the more] they are sometimes dragged down to lower things. (*Sermo* 47.28)

Notice he does not deny the holiness of the good; he calls them "the saints." But he does remark that it is a constant struggle for them to remain mindful of the source of their virtue. They must keep repeating, in the words Saint Benedict, extracts from Psalm 113, "Not to us, Lord, not to us, but to your name give the glory."

"The heavens proclaim the glory of God" (Ps 18:1) and "the whole earth is filled with God's glory" (Isa 6:3), although it can be perceived only through the eyes of faith. Whatever there is of beauty in creation we may affirm to be a refraction of the unseen God. Ultimately, however, according to the famous saying of Saint Irenaeus, "God's glory is the fully alive human being." God's real work is found in the creation, redemption, and divinization of human beings. We see something of God most clearly in those in whom this work has proceeded without resistance. It is in contact with the lives of the saints that we are touched most immediately by the mystery of God's presence and activity. There is an otherworldly quality about them that attracts and energizes us. According to the medieval Cistercians, holiness almost always becomes visible in the face of the holy person; there is a physical transformation. We are not speaking about effects comparable to those achieved by makeup and cosmetic surgery. Holiness works outward from the heart, reforming the whole body so that, despite age and decrepitude, it shows forth something of the goodness and kindness and beauty and accessibility of God. The glory of God has truly come to dwell in our land in the features of the saints. That is why we are more likely to be converted by contact with a holy person than by studying hundreds of books. The glory of God appears in human beings whom long contemplative practice has made fully alive.

This glory, shown forth in human beings, belongs to God and not to them, and this is why they keep on saying, "Not to us, Lord, not to us, but to your name give the glory."

In the same way, Paul the Apostle did not attribute anything of his preaching to himself but said, "It is by God's grace that I am what I am."

There is a growing trend these days for authors to include a lengthy list of acknowledgments at the beginning or end of their books. I am often bemused by these, especially when they include those who were simply hired for their services. Cynic that I am, I often wonder whether this is not just an elaborate form of political correctness rather than a sincere admission of indebtedness. The same holds for winners of Academy Awards and other forms of social recognition. Am I really expected to be gushingly grateful to the obstetrician who delivered me? In the event that I had not been successful, would these people whom I now acknowledge still have been the recipients of my thanks? Do I feel grateful only when things go well?

Gratitude is a beautiful human quality but it can easily be counterfeited. The most genuine form of gratitude is, it seems to me, not merely saying, "Thank you." It is a matter of mentally recomposing the whole narrative of my life to show more clearly the positive role that my benefactor has had in its evolution. I am truly grateful when the other person is an integral part of my self-image. If I were to speak about myself I could not but also speak about those to whom I am grateful—and this in hard times as well as when all runs smoothly. I would want to recount, with specifics, what they have been for me. I would understand these people to be an essential part of my story. This is why in the psalms one form of praise (so-called descriptive praise) is to describe what God has done in detail. God has created the world in all its beauty and intervened in the history of his people; God has made known to us the way to eternal life and has promised support and sustenance on our journey. This is why we praise God.

When it comes to my own life, it is easy to say, with Saint Paul, "It is by God's grace that I am what I am," without much more than a casual nod in God's direction. It is the kind of thing that good people are expected to say. It can have no more meaning than the jubilant sign of the cross soccer players from traditionally Catholic countries make when they score a goal. Words and gestures are one thing; inner conviction is something else.

Are we to limit our gratitude to those occasions when life seems to fulfill our expectations? When we see ourselves as winners it is easy to be generous in our praise of others and in our recognition of the gifts given by God. How is it at other times? It takes an extraordinary person to wake up each morning grateful for the gift of a new day, for the challenges, the sacrifices, the failures, and even the sins that it will bring. Our day-to-day life is mostly a mixed bag of blessings and burdens. To God be all praise for the blessings, but what about the moments when life is hard and no prospect of improvement is likely?

Gratitude to God is the fruit of faith, not the result of success, a sunny temperament, or the approval of others. We are grateful to God even when things go wrong because we have given assent to the proposition that "all things work together unto good for those who love God" (Rom 8:28). We admit that our judgment is not always right; when it seems to us that things have gone wrong, our faith asks us to believe that in God's sight there is a purpose. Saint Benedict quotes the psalm:

"It is good for me that you have laid me low . . . so that I may learn your commandments" (RB 7.54; Ps 118:71-73). God reveals himself to us just as much through failure as through success. Surely it is our experience that it is often easier to find God in hard times than when everything is brilliant. As Bishop Helder Camara wrote, "The Lord is there. He is far less likely to abandon us in hardship than in times of ease."

Praise of God walks or runs on two legs—the recognition of the magnanimity of God and the acknowledgment of our own difficulties and failures. The Latin word *confessio,* as used by Saint Benedict, spans both meanings. In the same way the *Confessions* of Saint Augustine and the *Confession* of Saint Patrick are not just the listing of sins committed, but the joyful recognition of the God who has delivered from the burden of guilt and sin and who is worthy of all thanks and praise.

"It is by God's grace that I am what I am"—warts and all. When I survey the landscape of my giftedness, it is not hard to praise God as its origin. There is, however, another side to my life that I hope will never intrude into public awareness. This is the shameful history of my selfishness and hardheartedness. For this I alone seem responsible. Indeed, this appears to be what Saint Benedict is saying in the fourth chapter of his Rule: "If he sees anything good in himself, let him refer it to God and not to himself. But let him know that the evil is always from himself and take responsibility for it" (RB 4.42-43). That makes sense at one level, but is it the whole story?

I do not want to appear to be ascribing to God the ugliness that is entirely my own creation. What I am saying is that the aspects of my life that are displeasing to me are not outside God's plan; they are designed to bring me to a fuller realization of the unconditional character of God's love. If I were all sunshine and light I could easily believe that God loves me because of my inherent goodness and that, in some way, I have made myself eminently worthy of that love. That seems to be a harmless enough delusion, but it is not. What do you think will happen when eventually I fall into some action that even I cannot deny, excuse, or rationalize? The logical conclusion will be that because of my misconduct God no longer loves me. My shame will quickly lead me to despair, as though God could be surprised and disgusted by the way human beings act.

Here's what the fourteenth-century English mystic Julian of Norwich has to say about this situation:

> For, in truth, we shall see in heaven for all eternity that though we have sinned grievously in this life, we were never hurt in God's love, nor were we ever of less value in God's sight. This falling is a test by which we shall have a high and marvelous knowing of love in God for ever. That love [of God] is hard and marvelous that cannot and will not be broken for our trespasses. . . . In love mercy allows us to fail somewhat, and in failing we fall, and in falling we die. . . . Our failing is full of fear; our falling is marked by sin; our dying is sorrowful. Yet in all this the sweet eye of pity never departs from us and the working of mercy never ceases. (*Revelation 14*, chaps. 61, 48)

It is true that it is by God's grace that we are what we are and by God's grace we have been preserved from countless calamities of our own making. Even though we fall short of our own hopes and expectations, it is by God's grace that we are what we are. God has a plan for us, of which we have only the sketchiest knowledge. Let us allow God to get on with the work and not delay its outcome either by taking credit for what meets with our approval or by becoming downcast when we are plunged into the mystery of our own resistance. "It is by God's grace that I am what I am." Whatever I have, I have received from God, and whatever I have become, it is part of the mystery of Providence. As always, the bottom line is this: I can never be beyond the pale of divine mercy.

And again he says, "Let the one who boasts, boast in the Lord."

Saint Benedict seems to be hammering this point hard. It is obvious that he does not want his disciples to become self-righteous Pharisees because of the good lives they are leading. He wants them to be ever mindful of how precarious all human virtue is. Just think of the self-confidence of Simon Peter at the Last Supper and how it was followed, just hours later, by his triple, that is to say, definitive, denial of Christ.

Nobody likes a boastful person even though we recognize that boasting is often the sign of someone who is profoundly insecure and is desperately seeking the approval and love of others. Fearful of how others might assess them, boasters try to preempt honest judgment by deluging their listeners with a torrent of propaganda. "I am the greatest," they repeat with many variations, while inwardly they feel quite the opposite. Meanwhile, many of those who hear them may be hoping fervently for some sort of disaster that might bring them to their senses.

The one in the New Testament who speaks most about boastfulness is Saint Paul. He sees boasting as an expression of an autonomy that weakens a person's total reliance on God—that is, it weakens faith. Those who think that religion is simply a matter of conforming to the precepts of the law, or perhaps so twisting the precepts of the law so that they are comfortable, have not yet learned the art of putting their trust in God, relying on God's mercy. They are locked into the schemes of self-perfection that they themselves have crafted. The end of such self-assurance can be only disaster. As Saint Ignatius of Antioch wrote to Polycarp, "The one who boasts has already come to nothing" (5).

Because we have nothing that we have not received (1 Cor 4:7), the truth is that there is no basis for boasting. Even though, by a careful selection of available evidence, we may be able to present ourselves to others as worthy people who have done a number of good things, this is not an accurate portrayal of our lives as a whole. There may be some simple persons whom we can deceive into thinking that we are better than we are, but the reality is that "all have sinned and have fallen short of the glory of God" (Rom 2:23). None of us has reached the standard God envisaged in creating us to his image and likeness; all of us have fallen short, whether this is public knowledge or not. In none of us is there any reason to boast.

The only real cause for boasting is the trouble we have experienced in life (Rom 5:13). There is ground for confidence when we have been called to participate by patience in the paschal mystery of Christ—when we share in the self-emptying process by which our redemption was accomplished. Boasting is self-filling—inflating ourselves beyond our merits in order to obtain the esteem of others. Following Christ in faith is the opposite of this; it is negating the power of self over our choices and actions and attitudes. To be Christian is to play our part in the paschal mystery, to supply in our own bodies whatever was lacking in the sufferings of Christ (Col 1:24).

This is why Saint Paul speaks about boasting in the cross of Christ (Gal 6:14). Paradoxically, the only thing that can give us confidence that we are on the right track is when everything seems to go wrong. When all our plans and projects proceed swimmingly, we easily lose our sense of dependence on God. Although we may continue with the outward forms of religion, we have no interior sense of the precariousness of our piety. It is only when things start to go wrong—as they inevitably will—that we feel helpless enough to turn to God as the only mainstay of everything we hold dear. Boasting comes from the sort of arrogance that blinds us to our frailty. It is untruth. When the unwelcome truth breaks into our complacency, it liberates us from this deadly ignorance and provides us with the opportunity to approach God with a humbler and more appropriate disposition.

Our only boast is that we have been called to participate by patience in the passion of Christ. Monastic life, in the view of Saint Benedict, is not some esoteric form of spiritual athleticism, whereby we train ourselves over a long period to perform at a higher level, one beyond our anticipated competence. Monastic life, like Christian life itself, is a matter of becoming ever more reliant on God's mercy and, therefore, ever more distrustful of our own achievements. Believe it or not, for some people, the only way to arrive at this point is to undergo some sort of more or less dramatic collapse.

Saint Benedict wants us to have the same dispositions as Saint Paul: our lack of boasting comes not from doubt of the gifts we have been given but from our recognition that they are gifts. In this case, thanksgiving pushes away any tendency to take pleasure in our present success and, paradoxically, to be content, and more than content, when hard times come.

Saint Paul speaks about how we have been enlightened by the knowledge of the glory of God revealed in the person of Christ, but then, glorying in his weakness, he continues: "We have this treasure in earthen vessels to show that this surpassing power is God's and not from us. We are troubled on every side but not crushed; confused but not desperate; persecuted but not abandoned; cast down, but not brought to nothing. We always carry around in our body the death of Jesus, that the life of Jesus may also be manifest in our body" (2 Cor 4:7-10).

To be living sacraments of Christ's presence in the world we need to leave aside our tendency to self-exaltation, to step aside so that the power of the living Christ may reach out to others through our littleness. There is nothing to boast about here. Our task is to stand aside and let Christ act. Again, Saint Paul is our instructor: "I want to know Christ and the power of his resurrection and to have communion in his sufferings, becoming conformed to him in his death so that, somehow, I may attain to the resurrection from the dead" (Phil 3:10-11).

Whence the Lord says in the Gospel, "The one who hears these my words and does them, I will liken to a wise man who built his house on rock."

Drawing his inspiration from the words of Jesus in the Gospel, Saint Benedict brings to the fore the theme of stability, a virtue characteristic of his Rule. There is a certain solidity about the way proposed by Saint Benedict. It is not flash. There is nothing particularly esoteric about the way of life he describes. For the most part it consists in the exercise of everyday virtues over a long period. This is probably why many laypeople, especially those with growing families, find that the spirituality of the Rule makes sense in very different situations. It is simply a matter of persevering in the plain teaching of the Gospels.

Those who have been in monastic life for a long time realize how important it is to lay firm foundations at the beginning. The first few years of monastic life are very important, just as are the formative first years of a child's existence. Much of the future shape of the prospective monk's career will be determined by what happens at this time. If someone gets into a habit of not taking seriously the monastic observance of the community, or begins to take shortcuts in one way or another, it will be only with great difficulty that change will be possible later on. It is a little like someone learning a new language. The only way to become proficient is total immersion. If the newcomer lives among compatriots for a few years, habitually reverting to the mother tongue and, for the rest of the time, speaking a kind of pidgin, never making a serious effort to learn the intricacies of the new language, it will be almost impossible to become fluent later on. Accent, intonation, and grammar will be complete mysteries, no matter how greatly better communication is desired.

This is why Saint Benedict sequesters newcomers and places them under the immediate care of an experienced elder while the process of discernment and stabilization is going on. The best indication of a monastic vocation is the reality of growth within a monastic environment. These first stages are crucial. One who is given, or who seizes by some form of extortion, the kind of liberty accorded to fully fledged monks will forever be at odds with the particularities of monastic observance, always straining against its necessary constraints, never acquiring the discipline that is the foundation of a creative life. It is not kindness to let newcomers run wild; it is dereliction of duty. Some temporary narrowness is necessary for the cultivation of the beliefs and values needed to follow the monastic path. In this way, good habits are established early that, with a bit of luck, will last reasonably intact for a lifetime.

But such training is no more than the scaffolding that keeps the building in place while construction continues. The real foundation is what endures once the building is complete and the scaffolding is removed. In the final analysis there is only one firm foundation to the lifelong living of monastic values—a deep, personal relationship with Jesus Christ that grows more intense as the years pass.

Christ is the rock on which Benedictine monastic life and spirituality is grounded; no doubt that is why Blessed Columba Marmion titled his groundbreaking book on monastic life *Christ, the Ideal of the Monk*. This affective relationship is more than fundamentalist flag waving, and it has to develop beyond a sentimental attachment to Jesus of Nazareth. It is, rather, a growing commitment to discipleship in the school of the Gospel, gradually absorbing Gospel values and, with great effort and many failures, learning how to practice them in daily life. It is by having the Jesus of the gospels as our master that we are gradually transformed, not by trying through mere willpower to change ourselves. The promise made in this verse refers to those who hear Christ's words and put them into practice; this is the pathway to that wisdom which is the solid foundation of a Christlike life.

This means, of course, that we are regular in applying ourselves to *lectio divina* in a spirit of faith and submission. In the Scriptures we learn Christ and, by conforming ourselves to him, we begin to develop an awareness of his presence in the events of daily life. This does not happen overnight but is the ordinary effect of long years of seeking to come closer to him through prayer and charity and, as we will see in the next verse, through surviving many dangers and storms.

Nothing can take the place of this solid foundation—nothing that we try to do ourselves, nothing that others may, in their pastoral solicitude, try to do for us. Christ is the rock on which we may hope to build a life that is pleasing to God. Christ is the foundation; Christ is also the one who builds on the foundation, as the psalm says: "Unless the Lord build the house, its builders labor in vain" (Ps 126:1).

34

"The floods came, the winds blew and assailed that house and it did not fall, because its foundations were on rock."

In recent years we have seen unnecessary deaths occurring in times of natural disaster because building codes were not enforced. As a result, when earthquakes or floods occurred, houses simply collapsed or were swept away. The enemy, in such cases, is a facile optimism that foresees no dangers. Those with more prudence recognize that in regions prone to earthquakes or flooding, special precautions are necessary. It may not happen this year or next, but with each passing year a potential disaster becomes more probable. This means extra labor and expenditure now in order to avert the consequences of a catastrophe that cannot be predicted with any certainty.

Monastic life is also prone to periodic crises, as is every form of Christian discipleship. These are not necessarily signs that something has gone drastically wrong; rather, they are the birth pangs that accompany the transition from a familiar pattern of life to a further stage of development. The fact that the person is advancing does not mean that there is less confusion or difficulty. Change is always a challenge, even when the change is for the better. Most of us want to be left alone in our rut; going onto something higher is often too much trouble—even if we are well-equipped to take the step. Saint Benedict warns the newcomer that the journey to God will involve passing through some hard country, and he wants the novice to be prepared to embrace what is hard and harsh—the *dura et aspera* (RB 58.8). This half-expectation of hard times ahead needs to be built into every beginning of more intense spiritual living. Only thus will the inevitable reversals that life brings have no power to shake our confidence, because our hopes are founded on solid rock.

Many ancient monastic writers were fond of citing the text of the biblical book of Ben Sirach (Sir 2:1), "Son, you have entered into the service of God. Stand strongly and prepare your soul for temptation." This is a good reminder that the service of God, in whatever form it takes, does not come easily to us. As soon as we make up our minds, under the influence of grace, to move in a certain direction, we immediately become aware of the attraction of staying where we are or of moving in a direction contrary to what we had decided. It is like trying to sail in a straight line while the prevailing winds continuously cause us to veer off course. The only way to avoid being troubled by temptations is, as Oscar Wilde remarked, to give into them immediately. If we decide on a good life, then we can expect to be continually confronted by possibilities of deviating from our ideal, slowing down our progress, or simply remaining where we are. If we accept that hard times will almost inevitably come, temptations will still be a bother, but they will no longer be a source of mental confusion. We will not have to ask ourselves, "Why am I tempted?" but simply accept the fact that for no one does human life always run smoothly. The apostle James goes even further than this when he writes, "Consider it a source of great joy, my brothers [and sisters], when all sorts of temptations befall you" (Jas 1:2). The words of the ancient sage are worth remembering: "Son, you have entered into the service of God. Stand strongly and prepare your soul for temptation."

Another much-quoted text was Job 7:1: "Human life on earth is military service." The less literal older Latin version was often substituted, "Human life on earth is temptation." Saint Gregory the Great had much to say on the storms that afflict human life and the continual subversion that undermines our noblest aspirations:

> Having forsaken the upright stance of the mind, we were bent over, and found ourselves subject to change through many channels. And so it happens that even if we seek to raise ourselves up to what is highest, we are quickly brought down to ourselves by the contrary promptings of our desire for continual change. We wish to stand upright in contemplation but cannot do so. We desire to control the direction of our thoughts but we are rendered impotent by the falls occasioned by our weakness. We bear unwillingly the burdens of our changeableness even though this was formerly so willingly embraced. (*Moralia* 8, 6.8; CChr 143, p. 86)

In other, simpler words we find it hard to persevere with our good resolutions. We make them in good faith, but they quickly weaken and fall off and we are back where we started, or even a bit worse off because of disappointment and discouragement.

Troubles will come from various sources: from emotional pressures; from illness; from our upbringing, our personal history, or our social situation; from the malice, ignorance, and weakness of others. Often our troubles come from our own willful resistance to good. All this is merely a normal result of being human. Saint Aelred of Rievaulx quotes the book of Ben Sirach in this connection: 'There is a heavy yoke on all the children of Adam from the day they came forth from their mother until the day of their return to the mother of all' (Sir 40:1). Pertaining to this unhappiness are all the miseries of this life: labors, pains, weariness, poverty, bereavement, all types of illness, trouble. O my brothers, who can number them all?" (*Sermo* 43.13). Perhaps this sounds like a gloomy assessment of what constitutes our life on earth, but there are few of us who have not experienced some of these troubles at least some of the time.

Troubles often make us lose heart; we become discouraged at the difficulties we experience and either give up our ideals, go back to what we were doing before, or distract ourselves by moving sideways and becoming involved in something useful or entertaining while, meanwhile, putting our deepest aspirations on hold.

We need to confront our troubles directly and try to determine to what extent we are complicit in our own difficulties. We suppose that storms and floods come always from outside ourselves, but often this is not so. It is always easier to cast the blame for hardship on other people or on external circumstances, but, more often than not, we contribute to our own misfortune. In such cases there is often something we can do to make things better.

If we take it for granted that storms will come and that at various junctures in our lives we will experience real hardship, then we can prepare ourselves to endure what comes and be ready to bounce back at the first opportunity. This requires a certain robustness in our spiritual life, the ability to pick ourselves up after a fall and continue the struggle. It requires the ability to recognize difficulties for what they are and to respond appropriately. Above all, it involves our being able to profit from our experience of what went wrong so as to make things better for the future. This is, in the final analysis, the cardinal virtue of prudence—learning from our mistakes what to avoid: the most typical mode of human learning.

Not that we will always be able to convert bad experiences into something good. Sometimes it will be simply a matter of endurance and stability. In such cases our response will be similar to what is required of a ship beaten by storm winds and a furious sea—a matter of battening down the hatches and waiting until the tempest abates and there is a great calm. Storms do not last forever, and even in the worst storms there are interludes of respite that enable us to catch our breath and continue the struggle.

To do this requires a measure of faith and the assurance that we are not utterly at the behest of the elements. The foundation of all endurance is our confidence in the lordship of Christ who will not allow us to be tempted beyond our powers to resist. It is also a matter of having confidence in the mercy of Christ whose love does not falter even when we fail and fall. Storms will come, but if our spiritual life is grounded on a real personal relationship with Christ, whatever goes wrong will not be the end of us.

Meanwhile, as the Scriptures often tell us, it is time to gird our loins and be prepared to do battle for Christ, the true king. We do not have to endure storms passively, like a rock in open country; we can stand up and fight the adversity. We can try to make things a little better. Confident of our solid footing and secure in the assurance that we can do all things in the power of Christ who strengthens us, we can face the storms and the floods without fear. This is because "God is our refuge and strength, an ever-present help in times of trouble. . . . The Lord of Hosts is with us, the God of Jacob is our fortress" (Ps 45:1, 7). If such is our house, it is built on solid rock; it will not fall.

Having finished this, the Lord waits for us every day to respond by deeds to his holy admonitions.

"Blessed are they who hear the word of God and keep it" (Luke 11:28). The way to happiness, as Jesus showed in the Gospel, is to welcome God's word so sincerely that it becomes a practical norm for everyday behavior. And this is the message to which Saint Benedict repeatedly returns in the Prologue. The act of listening is complete only when what is heard is internalized and then expressed in action. It is by deeds that we respond to God's holy admonitions.

The Lord's waiting for our response is a striking image. The Rule of the Master highlights the passivity of God by adding the note that God waits in silence for us to make some response to his call. The ball is in our court: God has revealed the way that leads to life, he has given us his grace to be our support, and now he waits for us to make a choice. As is said in the book of Deuteronomy, "Today I set before you life and death . . . choose life" (Deut 30:15-19).

The extraordinary image of God, the Maker of heaven and earth, patiently waiting for poor human beings to make up their minds is an anthropomorphic way of emphasizing the freedom of the human will and also the theological theme that God forces himself on no one. Saint Bernard of Clairvaux beautifully describes this mystery when speaking of the annunciation:

> The angel is waiting for an answer. We also, O Lady, upon whom the sentence of damnation piteously weighs, are waiting for a word of pity. . . . Poor Adam and his descendants, made exiles from paradise, beg you [to answer]. This is what Abraham, David, and the other holy fathers, who dwell in the region of the shadow of death, desire. The whole world, cast down at your feet, awaits [an answer]. . . . O Lady, answer with the word which the whole earth, the depths and the heights, await. Also the King and Lord of all, as much as he desires your beauty, desires also that you answer and give assent. (*Missus est* 4.8)

This dramatic scene, so powerfully portrayed, mirrors what happens in our own lives. We are presented with the prospect of doing good, of following Christ, of walking the way of discipleship. All this is laid out before us. The choice, however, is ours. The possibilities of good are merely possibilities until we make the decision and move forward into action. Heaven and earth await our response to God's invitation, whether it comes to us from an angel or by other more mundane channels.

It is not, however, a single choice that we must make. Saint Benedict reminds us that "the Lord waits for us every day to respond by deeds to his holy admonitions." It is daily fidelity to the divine call that is the engine that drives monastic life forward.

This sense that our commitment to the Gospel needs to be made not once in a lifetime but every day of our life is powerfully present in Saint Athanasius' *Life of Antony*, which had so much influence on later monasticism. Here are some quotations from that work; note how often the phrase "every day" occurs. Here is his fundamental principle, "*Every day* let us increase our zeal as if we were just beginning" (*Vita Antonii*

16.3). The faithful service of past years should not lead us into complacency so that we begin to relax our efforts:

> A servant would not dare to say "I worked yesterday, so I am not going to work today," seeing the work done in the past as a pretext for avoiding work in the days to come. But, as we read in the Gospel, in order to please his master and to avoid getting into trouble, he must show the same zeal *every day*. In the same way, we ought, *every day*, to persevere in the practice of asceticism, knowing that the Lord will not be indulgent because of what we have done in the past but will be angry with us because of what we neglect in the present. (VA 18.2)

Again.

> [Elijah] was zealous *every day* to present himself to God as one should appear in God's presence: pure in heart and ready to obey God's will alone (VA 6.12).

In order to remain vigilant Antony recommended to his disciples that they examine their daily behavior to see whether it conforms to their ideals and commitments: "*Every day* everyone should submit to reckoning their actions of the day and the night" (VA 55.7). Above all, Antony warned, by word and example, lest the concerns of daily life obscure the hope of heaven, lest forgetfulness of the future life allow us to become slack: "*Every day* [Antony] sighed, thinking of the heavenly abode, longing for it and considering human life ephemeral" (VA 45.1).

You will remember that Saint Benedict also wanted monks to desire eternal life and daily to keep their thoughts on the reality of death. As he wrote in chapter 4, "To desire eternal life with all spiritual yearning and to have the prospect of death daily before one's eyes" (RB 4.46-47). The *Life of Antony* has a similar emphasis: "[Antony] exhorted them not to relax their efforts and not to lose courage in their asceticism but to live *every day* as if they were about to die" (VA 89.4). Again:

> To avoid a loss of fervor, it is good to meditate on the saying
> of the Apostle, "I die daily." If we were to live *every day* as if
> we were about to die we would not sin. This is to say that
> *every day*, on rising, we should reflect on the fact that we
> may not last until evening; when we go to rest we should
> reflect on how we may never get up. By nature our life is
> uncertain and is measured out to us *every day* by Providence.
> If we have such an attitude and live *every day* accordingly,
> we shall not sin. We will desire nothing. We will have no
> resentments against others. We will not accumulate treasure
> on earth but, rather, will look ahead *every day*, to our death.
> In this way we will become detached and we will have noth-
> ing against anyone. (VA 19.2-4)

It is in the dailiness of our endeavors that monastic life
works its magic. The way to God proposed by Saint Benedict and the whole monastic tradition is ordinary, obscure,
and laborious. It makes up for its lack of drama, however, by
consistency and stability. It is in living in fidelity to the Gospel
every day, and every day responding by deeds to the Lord's
holy admonitions, that we make sure-footed progress on the
road that leads to eternal life.

36

**Because of this he has declared a truce during
the days of this life to give us the opportunity
to amend evils.**

The idea in this verse seems to be that God has declared
a sort of amnesty while we are on this earth to give us time
to get our affairs in order before we come to stand before the
court of divine justice. To us it may seem a curious concept;

no doubt it is one that occasions a measure of unease among those who forget that Saint Benedict's perspective on human life was different from ours. For the author of the Rule an exposition on the dynamics of monastic or spiritual life was impossible without taking into consideration the reality of divine judgment. For Saint Benedict, the ultimate sanction that keeps us on the straight and narrow is the prospect of being hauled up before God and, if found wanting, being thrown down to hell. This may not be one of our favorite topics for meditation, but it was an important truth for Saint Benedict, who keeps reminding the abbot that, though his discretionary power here on earth is near absolute, he also will have to render an account of all his decisions to the Judge of all. Saint Benedict firmly believes that it is the quality of our life here on earth that will determine our fate for all eternity.

A temporary amnesty to allow us to clean up our act before the hour of judgment is, therefore, a supreme manifestation of mercy. But, because the length of days allotted is unknown, it is also an encouragement to get working at once on the amendment of life.

Perhaps the best background to this verse is the parable of the fruitless fig tree in Luke 13. It follows on Jesus' ominous response to the news of various disasters that had taken the lives of innocent people. Uncompromisingly, Jesus says, "Unless you have a change of heart you too will perish in the same way." Not the kind of saying that we want to hear, but it is one that we should not ignore. Jesus goes on to illustrate what he means by a parable:

> Then Jesus told this parable: "A man had a fig tree, planted in his vineyard, and he went to look for fruit on it but found none. So he said to the person who took care of the vineyard, 'For three years now I have been coming to look for fruit on this fig tree and I have not found any. Cut it down! Why

should it use up the soil?' The man replied, 'Lord, leave it alone for one more year, and I'll dig around it and manure it. If it bears fruit next year, fine! If not, then cut it down.'" (Luke 13:6-9)

The purpose of having a fig tree and looking after it for years is that eventually it will bear fruit. The whole project is an investment. If it yields nothing, the obvious solution is for the owner to cut his losses and get rid of the useless tree and replace it with something else. Another parable, that of the wicked farmers who fail to pay their rent, makes the same point. And in the parable of the talents, the solitary talent is taken from the servant who buried it and given to one who already has plenty. For those who have there will be an abundance, but from those who fail to produce, even what they have will be taken away.

The message that Saint Benedict has taken from the New Testament is that there is a certain urgency in the matter of our conversion. Now is the time to begin producing the fruits that will endure for eternal life. This is probably why, in chapter 49, he quotes Saint Leo in saying that the life of the Christian or the monk should be a continual Lent: an intense time for taking stock of life, seeing what is wrong, and repairing the damage before it is too late.

We have been given an extended time on earth precisely in order to provide us with the opportunity of bringing our life into conformity with God's will, thus assuring our on-going growth and preparing us to receive the gift of eternal life. It is not time to waste in presumptuous procrastination. "Today if you hear God's voice, harden not your hearts." "Now is the time to rise from sleep." These are scriptural exhortations that Saint Benedict takes seriously. We have but a limited time to do on earth the good of which we are capable. Seize the moment because it may be shorter than you think. This is why, in the more apocalyptic sections of the New Testament, we are told to be vigilant, to remain on our guard, because we do not know the day or the hour of the Lord's coming.

The Second Epistle of Peter has a similar context that frames the exhortation to live a good life:

> Beloved, do not forget this. With the Lord a day is a thousand years, and a thousand years are a day. The Lord is not slow in fulfilling his promise, as some understand slowness. He is patient with you, not willing anyone to perish, but that all will come to repentance. But the day of the Lord will come like a thief. On it the heavens will disappear with a roar; the elements will be destroyed by fire, and the earth and everything in it will be laid bare. Since everything will be destroyed in this way, what kind of people ought you to be? It follows that you must live holy and religious lives. (2 Pet 3:8-11)

It is good to remember that this tradition is operating at the level of motivation; it is an attempt to get us moving on the way that leads to God by reminding us the time will come when we will not be able to change our ways even though we may wish to do so. It is not a particularly exhilarating thought. Nor does it have to be. It is simply a sober reminder of the reality that our life on earth will come to an end and with it our possibility of doing good. "Run while you have the light of life, lest the darkness of death overtake you."

This truth about humanity needs, however, to be balanced by the truth about God. God is not an impartial observer of our struggles but rather one who is actively involved not only in neutralizing the malign effects of our past failures but also in helping us to live more creative lives. And he does not limit the number of times he comes to our rescue. It is a continual and ongoing task! "The one who was compassionate forgave their wickedness and did not destroy them. Time after time God restrained anger and did not stir up rage, remembering that they were only flesh, a wind that passes and does not return" (Ps 77:38-39).

As the Apostle says, "Do you not know that the patience of God is leading you on to repentance?"

Living a spiritual life or following the monastic way requires such a sustained expenditure of energy that it is easy for us to come to the conclusion that we are the main players in this particular game. Of course we duly ask for, receive, and acknowledge the help of God, but, for all practical purposes, we carry on as though everything depends on us. The more we do this the more we are liable to become discouraged by the outcome. The spiritual journey is not reducible solely to factors that are under our own control.

God has a plan for us—not just a static blueprint, but a plan that is continually updated to accommodate the choices we make and the things that happen to us. We are easily conscious of the little dramas that punctuate our existence and the choices—large and small—that we make. We attribute great importance to these. But we rarely consider how Providence is shaping our lives. Understanding God's plan requires us to take a long view. As Winston Churchill once wrote about the study of history, "It is necessary to watch the tides and not the eddies."

One of the frustrating elements of God's manner of dealing with us is that, for our own ultimate good, we are not permitted uninterrupted progress. We would much prefer to follow a smooth upward curve that would take us to the top without drama or setback. But God has other plans. Our safe arrival at the gates of heaven is not predicated on a smooth journey. As is said in Acts 14:2, "We must go through many hardships if we are to enter God's kingdom." Hardships, setbacks, failures, sin: these are the means by which we are formed to become amenable to God's mercy.

In the third century, Clement of Alexandria wrote a book on Christ as our pedagogue. Christ is our master, our instructor, taking us from our rude, uncultivated state to a level of spiritual refinement that we cannot even imagine. Because we do not know where we are going, we do not know what roads lead to our destination. We have no alternative but to trust our guide.

All this is fine. There is, however, something else. Some things can be learned only by trial and error, of which the greater part is error. Our commitment to the right path is facile when it is the only path of which we have experience. It often needs a period spent off the path, struggling against the undergrowth, without any sense of the direction in which we ought to be traveling, confused and frustrated by our lack of progress. Then we begin to value a solid path that will take us to the desired destination.

God's providence allows us to go astray, sometimes seriously. Pope John Paul I had this to say on the matter: "I run the risk of making a blunder, but I will say it; the Lord loves humility so much that, sometimes, he permits serious sins. Why? In order that those committing these sins may, after repenting, remain humble" (*L'Osservatore Romano [Weekly Edition in English]* 37 [546: 14 September 1978], p. 8).

This is an idea that takes some getting used to. God's particular plan for us includes the probability that we will make a mess of things more than once in our lives, and thus it includes backup plans for our recovery and restoration. We are often tormented by our failure to live up to our self-contrived and perfectionist ideals, forgetting that God knows that we are "only flesh, a wind that passes and does not return." God's saving plan is not predicated on our sin-lessness. In fact, the opposite is the case. It includes remedies and restoratives for the times when our human limitations triumph over our idealistic spiritual ambitions.

The following text from Saint Gregory the Great explains how God withholds certain graces from those otherwise gifted so that they may maintain a sense of proportion about their achievements and not forget whence their gifts derive:

> The dispensation of almighty God is large. It often happens that those to whom he grants the greater goods are denied the lesser, so that their minds might always have something with which to reproach themselves. Hence, although they long to be perfect, it is not possible for them. They work hard in the areas where they have not been given the gift, and their labor achieves no result. In consequence they are less likely to have a high opinion of themselves in the areas in which they have been gifted. Because they are not able to be victorious over small vices and excesses, they learn that the greater goods do not derive from themselves. (Gregory the Great, *Dialogues* 3.14.12; SChr 260, p. 312)

"The dispensation of God," he says, "is large." God's unde-viating concern is to bring us safely to our heavenly home-land. To accomplish this God often has to subvert some of the conscious and unconscious barriers we erect to the fulfill-ment of his plan. Our relationship with God is important; the fulfillment of our own petty plans for our life is not so important. Often it will happen that our dreams and schemes will be frustrated, and God permits this to the extent that their abandonment serves the long-term purpose of our be-coming more dependent on the workings of grace. We are disappointed and saddened and even frustrated when we seem not to be able to live up to our own expectations. God, however, is sanguine about our failures. God is patiently lead-ing us to reframe our lives according to more wholesome principles through our experience of the ineffectiveness of our own efforts.

Some of us learn quickly to have complete confidence in the seemingly whimsical twists of Providence and so we are more relaxed in riding the waves that carry us beyond where we want to go. On the other hand, some of us are slow learners. We fight against reality and rebel when our plans come to nothing and then we become despondent because even our rebellion seems ineffectual. For such as these to be saved, God's spoiling interventions will need to be more intense and more frequent.

John Cassian gives a little commentary on the Lord's Prayer in his ninth *Conference*. In it he says that nobody can really say this prayer except one who is utterly convinced that all that happens in life is governed by Providence and who believes that whatever comes from the hand of God is good, even though it may seem otherwise. To pray well we need to have the firm faith that God is in charge of events, even when they seem not to conform to our expectations, even when our own life seems to be deteriorating, even when we are conscious of an intractable resistance to God's love. Meanwhile, like the father of the Prodigal Son, God is waiting patiently for us to turn back.

38

For the kind Lord says, "I do not want the death of sinners but that they may be converted and live."

God's will for us is that we change, because change is the best evidence of being alive. God's will is for us to loosen our hold on limited life in order to grasp more firmly a more abundant and lasting life. For most of us this means conversion, and conversion brings into our life an element of change that is not altogether welcome. It is important, however, to realize that the change willed by God is not the change that indicates nonacceptance of us as we are but that change foreseen by a creative vision that can perceive as-yet unrealized potentialities in us. In God's eyes there is no limit to what we can become if only we are willing to keep moving forward, not clinging to what has already been achieved but open to new and unexpected horizons. There is always scope for new and surprising growth. This is why Saint Benedict emphasizes the kindness of God who, out of love for us, does not wish us to continue with self-destructive or self-limiting behavior but to open ourselves up to the more abundant life that Jesus came to bring. We often think of conversion as being a change from a life of sin to a life of virtue; more often it is a matter of being called forth from our harmless comfort zone to take a less-traveled road into strange and unfamiliar territory.

It remains true, however, that we are all sinners—whether we are prepared to acknowledge it or not and however we choose to define sin. People of my generation usually consider sin as "any willful thought, word, deed, or omission against the law of God." We learned that definition by rote many decades ago in catechism class. In this approach, sin is viewed as a violation of God's laws: not only the Ten Commandments, but the natural law, the rules of ethics, the internalized conventions of the society in which we grew up, and the disciplinary regulations of the church. In such a perspective, conversion is understood as the move from disobedience to obedience, from rebellion to compliance, from negligence to diligence. With so many laws to observe from such an early age, no wonder many of our contemporaries were inclined to scrupulosity.

It seems that the idea of virtue as keeping the law and sin as breaking the law is firmly embedded in our consciousness. It is, certainly, one possible way of conceptualizing the appropriate relationship of the human being and God, but it is not the only way. I sometimes wonder how much the history of morality would have changed if, instead of the "ten commandments," we were given a list of "ten points that determine the health or sickness of the human person." Murder, adultery, and theft would have been seen as disabilities or illnesses needing a remedy rather than as actions worthy of punishment. In such an approach, our morality would have been framed by physicians instead of lawyers. Sin would have been seen as the work not of criminals but of those who are unwell, those who are burdened with some inherent debility that makes it a struggle to achieve the good of which they are capable and that makes them chronically prone to backsliding into unproductive and destructive behavior.

This was certainly the view of Aelred of Rievaulx, who understood the various vices as burdens that oppress us, as a heaviness that weighs down the lightness and joy of being human. He regarded sin more with pity than with blame. Sin is certainly an offense against God. It is a violation of an ethical code; it is a crime against our neighbor and a weakening of the fabric of society. It is all these things. But it is also a crime against ourselves. All sin is inherently self-destructive because it defiles and debilitates what has been created by God to become beautiful and strong. A muscle that is abused ceases to operate naturally and causes pain; sin is an abuse of our humanity that—despite transitory gratification—will ultimately cause us pain.

It is surely significant that Jesus, in promulgating the new covenant in the Sermon on the Mount, presented it not as a law but as a way to happiness. Happy are the poor and the meek and the persecuted! The paradoxical path proposed by Jesus is the only way to complete human fulfillment. Oddly enough, it is by letting go that we acquire, by living humbly that we become strong, and by dying that we enter into limitless life. The way to ultimate human happiness is to make our choices in the light of ultimate values—even though they seem to run counter to our short-term interests. In this way we are liberated from the tyranny of the present and able to shape our lives with a view to our final destination.

Those unable to orient themselves according to ultimate realities are the prey of whatever forces the present moment exerts. Their freedom is limited by their circumstances and their history. The wretchedness of those trapped in a habit of sin is that they know full well that their conduct is self-destructive, but they do not have the skill or the energy to escape. Obsessions, compulsions, addictions, habits—all of these drive us to behavior that ultimately makes us unhappy, but we cannot find within ourselves the capacity to change our lives.

Before we come to the point of conversion, there is a long period of dissatisfaction. We become more and more unhappy about the way that we live but cannot see our way clear to making any change. We have not yet reached the tipping point, even though a momentum is slowly developing. Not every time is right for conversion. The unhappier we become with what we are at present causes us to become gradually detached from our uncreative living and slowly turns us around toward a better way of life. The grace of God is infinitely patient. It bides its time until we are ripe for the picking. Whether God intervenes now to make a change in our lives or holds back until a more propitious moment, what is done is done with a view to our salvation. God is not inactive or forgetful. If there is a delay, it is a tactical delay, waiting for us to arrive at the point where change becomes feasible.

Brothers, since we have asked the Lord about those who dwell in his tent and we have heard the instructions for dwelling [in that place], we have to do the duty of one who dwells there.

A new section of the Prologue begins at this verse. Saint Benedict, following the Master, concludes his reflection on the biblical texts and moves onto the more practical matter of their implementation. It is not enough for us to be mere hearers of the word: we must understand it, apply it to our own lives, and begin to follow its injunctions in our daily behavior.

We see coming to the surface here the idea that there is not much point asking for advice or guidance unless we are prepared to follow it. We all know people who constantly seek counsel from a variety of sources and never follow any of it. Sometimes they play one advisor against another; sometimes they merely keep asking until they find the answer that suits them. Others, as Jean-Paul Sartre noted, choose their counsel by their choice of counselor. Sincere seeking of advice requires us to listen carefully to what is said, to take it into consideration, and to be willing to put it into practice. If this is true of human counsel, it is even more important when we approach God. God does respond to our prayer, if we listen closely, but it is not always the response that we want or expect.

Earlier, I referred to a favorite text of mine from the sixth-century Palestinian father, Dorotheos of Gaza. It reminds us that God never disregards our prayers when we sincerely ask for guidance. But, there is a catch. God has unexpected ways of communicating his will to us, and we will be able to perceive it only if we are truly genuine in our seeking of guidance. Dorotheos draws an example from the book of Numbers to remind us that if God could speak to the prophet Balaam through a donkey, there is no shortage of ways in which he can get a message through to us. This is what he wrote:

> In the same way do not ponder what you have to do if you have no one from whom you may ask [counsel]. God will not abandon any who wholeheartedly seek to know God's will in truth. God shall in everything show them the way according to his will. For those who turn their heart to [discovering] God's will, God will enlighten a little child to speak the will of God. (*Instruction* 5 #68; SChr 92, p. 264)

God will speak to us somehow—even if it involves making use of surprising channels of communication. But we must be prepared to listen since God may not speak through the storm or the earthquake or the fire but only through the subtle movement of a silent breeze (see 1 Kgs 19:11-12). If we are to hear the divine voice speaking to us, we must imitate God who does not make assessments according to outward appearances but looks into the heart (see 1 Sam 16:7). Sometimes God's saving word comes to us from an unlikely source: from the mouth not of a friend but of an enemy. In every case, however, we need to listen well.

Listening implies obedience. In many languages the two words are related. Part of the necessary disposition in coming to *lectio divina* is our being willing to put into practice whatever we encounter in our reading. We submit to God's word with the obedience of faith. This submission needs to be present before we begin to read, before we know what God may be asking of us today. We pray that we may be led, guided, encouraged to move forward without knowing our final destination. This cannot be a selective response. It must be wholehearted and courageous. Saint Paul states this unequivocally:

"As God is faithful, our message to you is not 'Yes and No.' For in the Son of God, Jesus Christ, who was preached among you by me, Silvanus, and Timothy, there was no 'Yes and No,' but in him there is [only] 'Yes'" (2 Cor 1:18-19).

If our desire for God, our desire to experience the presence of God, our desire for union with God, is wholehearted, then it will express itself in our willingness to do whatever it takes to be worthy to receive God's gift of Self. It is not that our energetic exertions are sufficient to achieve our goal, but they make us ready to receive God's gift, partly by systematically reducing and eliminating the obstacles to union with God and partly by developing in us a higher degree of spiritual sensibility so that we may perceive the Spirit's actions in the depths of our being.

Halfheartedness is a serious impedance to spiritual progress. It is surely not without significance that Jesus gave as the first commandment, "Love the Lord your God with *all* your heart, with *all* your soul, and with *all* your mind" (Matt 22:37). The whole endeavor of spiritual living is meant to reduce the dividedness of our interior being and for us to be single-hearted in our seeking of God. As Jesus said, "No one can serve two masters" (Matt 6:24).

This means that our discipleship cannot be a part-time commitment, quarantined in certain religious moments, with the rest of our life left untouched. To be merely a Sunday Christian is a mockery of religion and of God. As followers of Christ we are always on duty; there should be no segment of our activity that is uninfluenced by our commitment to Gospel values. Even though it is true that, for much of our lives, our commitment will vary in intensity and that our efforts to be Christlike will be spread very thinly, it is better that our whole life is a little seasoned by faith than that there is too much religion in some areas and too little in others. We should make the effort to open up every corner of our life to the saving presence of Christ, so that by the gift of his grace we may slowly become less conflicted, more integrated, and more fully ourselves. As Christ becomes more present in everything we do, we also will be more present in our actions; they will manifest more fully the imprint of who we are and be true expressions of the renewed person we have become in Christ.

Saint Benedict is insistent that we translate our aspirations into practical behavior. If we want to dwell in the Lord's tent, we have to comply with the conditions for this possibility. We have asked the Lord and have heard the response. Now is the time for us to begin implementing the instructions we have received. No excuses! No complaints! "Now is the hour for us to rise from sleep. . . . If today you hear God's voice, harden not your hearts" (RB Prol. 8-10).

I note that an early Cistercian manuscript of the Rule, Dijon No. 114, adds to this verse the promise, "and so we will be heirs of the kingdom of heaven." This is, as John Cassian notes in his first *Conference*, the ultimate goal of monastic life and of all spiritual striving. If you wish to enter God's kingdom, here is the road to take; if you follow it, you can be sure that one day you will arrive at the goal of all your desiring. To make sure of entering heaven we are invited to pursue, already here on earth, a heavenly life, a life that is marked by the imprint of Christ's love.

40

Therefore our hearts and bodies must be prepared to serve under the instructions of holy obedience.

Since the sixteenth century, especially in those cultures secretly influenced by Cartesian dualism, there has been a tendency to consider the spiritual life entirely as a matter of interior feelings, states, and actions. The disembodied spirituality that resulted often concentrated excessively on the conscious experience of individuals and neglected not only the deeper stirrings of the human spirit but also the everyday role played by sacramental practice, good works, and community life. The spiritual life was considered almost as a private affair between oneself and God, and meditation became a means of exercising control over one's life rather than a channel by which one could open oneself to be surprised by God. Liturgy and contemplation became polar opposites.

Traditional monastic life, on the contrary, emphasized the importance of arriving at a harmony of body and soul, both working together toward the same goal. A monk prayed and a monk worked; it was expected that the bodily work he did for the support of the community would be permeated by prayer. In his prayer his body was active by its changing postures and its stillness. In his chapter on humility Saint Benedict sees this quality of mind as manifested by the combination and interaction of both interior and exterior expressions: "the sides of the ladder are the body and the soul" (RB 7.9). And when the monk reaches the summit of humility his submission to God becomes visible by his bodily stance, no matter where he is or what he does: "The twelfth step of humility is that a monk always manifests humility to those who see him not only in his heart but also in his body. That is, at the Work of God, in the oratory, the monastery, the garden, on a journey in the fields, or anywhere else. Whether he sits, walks, or stands, his head is to be always bowed and his eyes fixed on the earth" (RB 7.62-63).

This picture of the near-perfect monk indicates just how holistic was Saint Benedict's vision of human nature. Years of practice do not turn the monk into some kind of ethereal being, more at home in heaven than on earth. On the contrary, though his thoughts may be directed heavenward, his feet remain firmly on the ground. Growth in spirituality means not greater separation or alienation from the body but the more complete integration of body and soul and their harmonious cooperation. Throughout the monk's life, as envisaged by Saint Benedict, body and soul work together so that in all things God may be glorified. God is glorified both by the act of standing and reverently bowing at the doxology (RB 11.3) and by refraining from avarice in the monastery's commercial undertakings (RB 57.9). The monk's worship of God in the liturgy is supplemented by the liturgy of life, doing the ordinary tasks of humdrum daily existence under the eye of God and in a spirit of reverence and thanksgiving.

Like Saint Benedict, Saint Aelred is utterly convinced that we need bodily observances, such as fasting, hard work, and keeping vigil, if we are to make much progress on the road that leads to eternal life. He writes, "They are badly deceived who, while they are still living in this mortal body, think that they do not need bodily exercises. . . . What I wish to insist on is that you cannot come to this point [of contemplation] through slackness or indolence but by labors, vigils, fasts, tears, and contrition of heart" (*Sermo* 34.3, 29).

Labors, fasts, vigils. For Saint Aelred, these are the means by which the transformation of the human being is accomplished and by which the person is prepared to receive the gift of contemplative union with God. They are also a practical expression by which we signal our determination to give priority to our search for God over other more useful and, perhaps, more gratifying activities.

Especially in the early stages of the monastic or spiritual journey it is worthwhile giving attention to achieving a measure of self-control in food, sex, alcohol consumption, and sleep; to diligence in practical tasks; and to the avoidance of aggression and envy in everyday relationships. Living thus provides a good foundation for progress toward a more conscious experience of union with God in prayer. Without such a basis, efforts to pray will often be bootless. We will come up against a solid wall because our interior sentiments are at odds with our bodily behavior.

A certain training in spiritual living is necessary if our hearts and bodies are to be fully engaged in the service of God. Saint Benedict sees this training as coming from participation in the common life of the monastery. For those who do not have this possibility, it is probably useful to formulate a flexible rule for themselves that will make it easier for them to persevere in doing the things that will work toward their long-term spiritual advantage.

Such a preparation of heart and body must be designed in such a way that it does not come under the control of self-will. Nearly every mystical tradition insists that those who begin this journey must be prepared to submit themselves to a discipline of life that will break the tyranny of self-will. We are called to self-transcendence; we will never make any progress in that direction unless we are willing to yield some measure of control. How can we plot a course to transcend our limits when we have no experience of living beyond these limits?

Our willingness to live under the guidance of a rule and abbot and in the context of a community is a sterling means of ridding ourselves of the burden of self-will. In many monastic texts the word "obedience" means more than mere compliance with commands given, the term serves as a kind of shorthand for the full range of monastic obligations. So, to prepare our hearts and bodies that we are able to enter into a contemplative relationship with God is simply to give ourselves willingly to the everyday demands of monastic life—to give ourselves generously to the observances that Saint Benedict prescribes in the Rule—"not tentatively, not reluctantly, not tepidly or with murmuring or expressions of unwillingness" (RB 5.14).

As far as Saint Benedict is concerned, there is nothing mysterious about the way that leads to the more complete experience of God. It is simply a matter of persevering with good zeal in the community life of worship, prayer, study, reading, work, and fraternity; accepting communal standards of poverty and simplicity; and allowing ourselves to grow in love as the years pass. This is the service of God that allows us to grow spiritually; this is the area in which we engage in spiritual warfare. It is by these means that our bodies are trained and our hearts are expanded so that the grace of God may work its wonders more fully in us.

41

For what is less possible for us by nature, let us ask the Lord that he may provide it for us by the help of his grace.

Throughout the Prologue, Saint Benedict is insistent on our using our best efforts to arrive at our chosen goal and the fulfillment to which God calls us. We need self-knowledge to know our contrary tendencies. We need wisdom in knowing how to neutralize their influence over us. We need courage to engage in spiritual warfare—resisting temptation and choosing what leads to life. We need constancy to persevere in our journey, especially when the going is hard and the outcome seems dubious. Above all, however, we stand in need of God's grace, which is given especially to those who ask for it.

In the early days of the spiritual life, when there seems to be much that needs doing, it is relatively easy to apply ourselves to the task of self-improvement. For a while we seem to make good progress, and we wonder why such a fuss is made about the challenges of spiritual living. As with infants, growth from month to month and from year to year is readily discernible. But just as the external growth of adults ceases, as the years pass, apparent growth in spiritual life slows down and often seems to go in reverse once we pass beyond the initial stages. I say "apparent growth" because appearances are deceptive. What is happening is that we grow in self-knowledge and so are able to see more clearly the liabilities we carry and our deeply ingrained resistances to the action of God in our life.

The realization that we are still far from the ideal does not usually come as a peaceful epiphany; more often it is experienced as a shock that shatters our complacency as it exposes the deep inconsistencies that were concealed beneath our initial bouts of piety. God acts like a surgeon who tries to build up the general health of the body before submitting it to the trauma of the scalpel. So God allows us to get started in our life of devotion and good works, perhaps to make some significant decisions, before holding a mirror before our eyes to allow us to see how necessary it is for us to undergo radical and ongoing surgery. When the time for cutting away rank growth comes, there is no avoiding it.

Unless we are completely obtuse, in the course of a long life there are many experiences that allow us to come face-to-face with our limitations. This happens most effectively when we are confronted with our failings and, particularly, those that occur in areas that have the most profound meaning in our lives. We do not really mind failing in our knowledge of the geography of Mozambique or failing to resist a second slice of chocolate cake. Such mishaps do not mean much to us. But when, through our own willful weakness, ignorance, or malice we make a mess of something to which we are dearly committed, then we are cast down. We are disappointed in ourselves because we have failed to rise to a challenge that we believed was well within our power to meet.

If there is question of the spiritual life, our failures often derive from the fact that probably we have overestimated our power to succeed in bringing to completion whatever plan on which we had set our hearts. It was probably an exercise in self-improvement designed to make us more acceptable in our own sight. No doubt we also underestimated the depth of our resistance to God's plan for our further progress. The greater our illusory self-confidence, the more devastating our collapse.

Such disasters play an important role in detaching us from schemes of holiness that have more to do with self-will than with God's gracious intentions in our regard. The failure of our own plans clears the way for the implementation of God's plans. We come to the point of realizing that our dream cannot be fulfilled on the basis of our own resources. We need the help that comes from God. We need grace; we need the active presence of the Holy Spirit.

When we recognize our inadequacy, then we begin to learn to pray. Prayer is born out of our realistic self-knowledge, and without self-knowledge prayer is merely pious playacting before God. As Saint Augustine says, "Because I am human I am weak; because I am weak I pray." Being at the end of one's tether is a good place to move more fully into prayer.

God is at work to bring us to such life-giving self-knowledge. In a necessary dialectic of presence and absence, our spiritual life passes through highs and lows, each state throwing light on a truth about ourselves. We are, at the same time, sinful and redeemed, loved by God and hateful to ourselves, drawn to what is highest and addicted to what is lowest. By becoming aware of our inward polarities we learn by experience that we cannot scale the Lord's holy mountain on our own merits; we need God's help. When we begin to call out for that help, real prayer is generated within us.

Listen to what Saint Bernard of Clairvaux has to say about this matter:

> For people who are spiritual, or rather for those whom the Lord intends to make spiritual, this process of alternation

goes on all the time. "God visits by morning and subjects to trial." The just person falls seven times, and seven times gets up again. What is important is that the fall occurs during the day so that such people see themselves falling, and know when they have fallen, and want to get up again. So they call out for a helping hand, saying [in the words of the Psalm]: "O Lord, you made me splendid in virtue, but then you turned away and I was overcome." (*Super Cantica* 17.2)

Notice the sequence of events: God seems to withdraw; the person falls, recognizes the fact, and then calls out for a helping hand. The key moment is recognizing the need for assistance. "I cannot do this on my own; I need help." Of course, help from God is always forthcoming, but we need to be willing to receive it. It is only to the extent that we come to the end of our own resources and are overcome by our inability to do what needs to be done that we are open to receive God's ever-present help. Bernard returns to this theme in another text:

God is revealed to us for our salvation through such an experience and it follows this order. First of all we perceive ourselves to be in dire straits; then we cry out to the Lord and we are heard. Then God will say to us, "I will free you and you shall honor me." Thus, in this way, self-knowledge is shown to be a step in the direction of knowledge of God. (*Super Cantica* 36.6)

Prayer comes forth from our recognition of our need for God; for most of us this follows the enforced recognition of our own limitations. It is easy enough for us to have an intellectual appreciation of the necessity of grace in spiritual life; discovering this experientially is more painful, but it has to happen. And when it does happen we will find that prayer comes readily to our hearts and to our lips, simply because there is no other hope for us except in the ever-present mercy of God. What is less possible for us by nature, let us ask the Lord that he may provide it for us by the help of his grace.

42

And if we flee the punishments of hell, because we wish to arrive at unending life,

Just in case we had forgotten, Saint Benedict once more frames our present life in terms of the choice between heaven and hell. The way we live now is going to have a bearing on our future mode of existence. It is important here to leave behind popular images of harp-playing angels and fiery demons wielding pitchforks. Heaven is the state of being fully open to the more abundant life that Jesus came to offer us; hell is simply our freely decided refusal to take up that offer, obstinately sulking in a corner, like the elder brother in the parable of the Prodigal Son, instead of celebrating the generosity of God in the banquet halls of heaven.

It is, of course, one of the mysteries of our human condition that we can find ourselves in a situation where we voluntarily choose what we know will make us miserable. Sometimes we choose short-term gratification even though it involves long-term diminishment. For example, we may cut short our education even though we know that we are depriving ourselves of the possibility of a more fulfilling career, or we may engage in some form of substance abuse, fully aware of its destructive consequences. More puzzling still is when we deliberately refuse to go further along a path that will enhance our life experience—out of routine, timidity, fear, or sheer obstinacy. We choose the less promising option, as if we enjoy the prospect of being miserable. We may excuse ourselves or blame others but the reality is, more often than we care to admit, that we are the cause of our own unhappiness. The choices that we freely made were not life-giving.

The freedom of the human will is an impenetrable mystery, but its practical effects are well-known to us from everyday experience. We cannot make another person's choices. We can offer advice and admonition, but the choice is not in our hands. We have to step back and wait while the will comes to a decision. Even God does not interfere with human freedom. We may live in a community that sustains right judgments, we may be given the wisdom to know what is right and what is good, our will may be strengthened by grace, yet the possibility always remains that we can say no to what is life-enhancing and give our assent to what ineluctably will lead to self-destruction. The doctrine of heaven and hell—whatever the imagery we use to explain it—is a necessary corollary of the affirmation of the freedom of the human will.

Of course, since the advent of psychoanalysis and the recognition of the degree to which our choices are influenced by factors of which we are unaware, we have been a little less ready to characterize every option we take as perfectly free. We are influenced and, to some extent, conditioned by many aspects of our personal history for which we are not personally responsible. I do not know exactly why my favorite color is my favorite color or why I enjoy some foods and abominate others. I have only recently become aware of why certain incidents and attitudes automatically trigger deep resentment in me. There is much I do not understand about why I make the choices that I do. In many trivial everyday options I fly by autopilot, leaving many matters to be decided without much personal involvement on my part. This is the choice I make; if it is not important I do not spend much energy on it. But the fact remains that, in more significant situations, when it comes to deciding what actions I should take to respond to these automatic feelings, it is I who make the decision. Based on conscious beliefs and values, I choose to do this or omit that. I am attracted to one alternative, but whether I am driven on by the attraction or step back to allow reason to make an assessment I will follow, that is my choice. I am responsible for the choice, for the action or omission, and for its reasonably predictable consequences. I am, in many matters, a sufficiently free agent. Yes, unconscious forces push me in particular directions but I still have the capacity to slow down my instinctive attraction, to step back and consider the options and to select among them. If I am mindful of my overriding priorities in life, and willing to accept the grace of God, the choice I make will be a good one. It will be life-giving.

The integrity of daily choices is an age-old challenge that confronts every religious person. We remember how it is expressed in the well-known text from Deuteronomy:

> See, this day I set before your face life and good, death and evil. For I command you this day to love the LORD your God, to walk in his ways, and to keep his commands, decrees, and judgments; then you will live and increase, and the LORD your God will bless you in the land you are entering to possess. But if your heart turns aside and you are not obedient, and if you are drawn away to bow down to alien gods to serve them, I declare to you this day that you will certainly be brought to nothing. (Deut 30:15-18)

Making life-enhancing choices is largely a matter of slowing down the process of choosing, allowing myself to be motivated not only by the onrush of present impressions but by more permanent and, perhaps, less immediate priorities. This means seeing each step I take as part of a lifelong journey and not simply as one of a disjointed series of separate steps: not an isolated moment but part of the flow of temporal life that begins at birth and continues until death. We instruct children to look left and right before crossing a busy street. We should do likewise. We are wise if before any significant decision we look backward over what we have learned in years past and we look forward at where we hope to be going in the years ahead.

Every choice—even the minor ones—should reflect the permanent beliefs and values by which we shape our life. Listen to what the prophet Jeremiah wrote: "This is what the LORD says: 'Stand at the crossroads and look; ask for the ancient roads, ask where the good road is, and walk in it, and you will find rest for your souls'" (Jer 6:16).

Equally, every choice should reflect our future. This means, as Saint Benedict will remind us in the fourth chapter, desiring eternal life with all spiritual yearning (RB 4.46). But he then reminds us that living with an eye on eternity involves keeping death daily before our gaze, because death is the means by which we pass over into eternity (RB 4.47). Our life will come to an end and we will be subject to judgment. If we wish to arrive at unending life, now is the time to start choosing life in all we do. If we wish to flee the punishments of hell, now is the time to start avoiding self-destructive choices. The grace of God calls us to walk the road that leads to eternal life, but whether we choose to pursue this path, for all practical purposes, depends on us. Today I set before you life and death: choose life.

43

then, while there is opportunity and we are in this body, and there is opportunity to complete [these tasks] by this light of life,

The verb that I have translated as "there is opportunity" is *vacat*, which suggests being disengaged or empty, free for something, available. This usage is not an indication that Saint Benedict considers this life to be a perpetual vacation, but rather it shows that he sees our time on earth as a moment of opportunity, a chance to take a step forward that may not continue indefinitely. We have nothing else to do that is so important as responding to the call of the Lord, not merely by an immediate notional assent, but, more especially, by an ongoing and real assent expressed through our manner of living.

We are rather used to believing that the way ahead in the spiritual or monastic life is to be doing lots of good works, to be active and busy about the practice of virtue. Goodness seems like a matter of generous giving. It is easy for us to forget such values as silence, stillness, and receptivity. All that happens to advance our spiritual life is a gift from God that depends less on what we do for God and more on what God does for us. Our best qualities are those we have received, not those we have manufactured for ourselves. Our capacity to welcome such gifts depends in large measure on our openness, our willingness to be changed, the degree of our disengagement from our private plans in order to be drawn into something greater than ourselves.

This is probably why the concept of leisure receives such emphasis in monastic tradition. The leisure to which I am referring is not a matter of having a holiday from obligations or from hard work but, rather, the freedom to be fully engaged with what matters most in whatever we do, so that what, in the depths of our being, we are and what we desire to become are fully expressed in whatever external works we perform. In other words, there is more emphasis placed on the subjective disposition of the worker than on the objective productivity of the work. This is why the Desert Fathers liked simple work such as weaving baskets out of reeds, because while providing a means of support and keeping their hands busy, it provided the occasion for their spirits to soar aloft. The same is true of the repetitive agricultural tasks beloved of monks of a previous generation and now, it seems, rendered unfeasible by modern farming methods.

Throughout Saint Benedict's Rule there is special attention paid to the quality of a monk's actions. When he speaks of monastic life as offering the opportunity to do now the things that will have a permanent and positive effect on our final outcome, Saint Benedict is not speaking merely of the list of good works to be done, as he does in chapter 4. The life he envisaged was a life in which it would be possible not only to add to the *quantity* of our good works but, more especially, to enhance the *quality* of whatever we do—to act mindfully, with the right intention, out of good zeal. This is why he does not wish the monk to be overburdened by the work to which he is assigned, as though the work were more important than the worker. Work done in moderation is more likely to be mindful than work that leaves no space for anything beyond itself.

The idea of spiritual progress as a gradual change in the quality of our life and experience is worth pondering. It is not so much a matter of doing more good deeds and fewer bad deeds and keeping a numerical tally of how we are doing. It is more a question of qualitative change; we do what we do, whatever it is, with a pure intention, with a care for justice, and in a spirit of love. Then what we do, whatever we do, is a noble work. This means that the value of our life is measured less by the importance of the tasks that we are given than by our personal radiance in daily duties done in love. I suppose this attitude could be termed a pursuit of excellence, but, allow me to repeat, it is an excellence that is measured not by external criteria but by its inherent innocence and goodness. Jesus said that giving a cup of cold water with the right disposition was sufficient for salvation (Matt 10:42). The "little way" enunciated by Saint Thérèse of Lisieux is really the only way. We go to God by a path that is ordinary, obscure, and laborious.

We allow our lives to be changed by stepping back from a headlong rush into schemes of self-improvement and giving ourselves room for maneuvering. Now is the moment of opportunity when we can realign our lives more fully with God's plan through conscientious reflection and meaningful action. But the key to further progress is thoughtful disengagement. The freedom about which Saint Benedict speaks has as its principal obstacle the conflicting agenda that we set up for ourselves. The plans that we have for our future, from wherever they come, are the most powerful disincentives to our being available to follow a more excellent way.

Now, then, is the time for us to avail ourselves of the space and freedom that this life affords to consider our call, our present response to that call, and the fact that there is only a short interval left to us to reach the goal to which we have been invited. As elsewhere in the Prologue, Saint Benedict injects a note of urgency into his reflections. At this moment we have the opportunity to be converted; there is no guarantee that this period of grace will go on indefinitely. Quite the contrary, we know that our life on earth will end and with it the opportunity to open ourselves more fully to God.

As life spans lengthen, we are beginning to realize that our capacity for conversion diminishes with our gradual decline in bodily and mental vigor. The brain becomes less able to countenance alternatives, change becomes abhorrent, and sometimes pain blots out all awareness of everything except itself. This is something that the thirteenth-century Cistercian John of Forde clearly recognized. Here is what he wrote:

> Indeed, excessive pain, like a stormy winter that precedes death, allows us to think of scarcely anything except its own unremitting severity. There is no place for being sorry because pain fully occupies the person's mind and thought. The soul bidding farewell to this life is like someone on the Sabbath; not permitted to do any meritorious work but able

only to do nothing. To do nothing, that is, that might be of profit, meanwhile [suffering] from whatever afflicts, upsets, and tortures. (*Super Cantica* 53.7; CChrM 17, p. 376)

Not a very cheerful text but a good reminder that there is spiritual spring cleaning to be done and that it is better done today than tomorrow. Or, as Saint Benedict said earlier in the Prologue, "Run while you have the light of life lest the darkness of death overtake you" (RB Prol. 13).

44

there is a need to run and do now what will profit us in perpetuity.

"Run while you have the light of life lest the darkness of death overtake you" (RB Prol. 13). We have already noted that Saint Benedict seems to like the image of running to indicate a level of enthusiasm for the task undertaken. Saint Augustine famously wrote, *Cantare amantis est* (Singing is typical of one who loves). Equally, perhaps, we could say, *Currere amantis esti* (Running is typical of one who loves). We cannot imagine Romeo dragging himself wearily through Verona to make his appearance beneath Juliet's balcony; running is more typical of one who loves, of one who desires. This is how Saint Benedict wants us to make our way along the road that leads to eternal life.

I suppose all of us have bad days in which everything we are asked to do seems like an insupportable burden. But even beyond that, with our legacy of seeing God's self-revelation as "the law," it is almost impossible for us to view the means of a more abundant vitality except in terms of obligations imposed. The problem with this approach is that for every obligation there is an equal and opposite reaction. We try to wriggle out from whatever is obligatory because we feel that it is an impediment to the freedom of our self-expression; we hate to think that we are jumping through hoops not of our own making. If we fall into the trap of perceiving monastic life or the spiritual life as a series of external imperatives— laws, regulations, obligations—we will almost certainly come to resent them, no matter how intellectually convinced we are of their value.

Yes, Saint Benedict is writing a rule; he is laying down the law. But if we cannot see beyond the text's prescriptiveness we will probably adopt a minimalist attitude toward its observance. If we feel that any obligation is a threat to our spontaneity, it is unlikely that we will run along the road to which Saint Benedict points. At best we will walk complaining, perhaps dragging ourselves along by sheer willpower or fear of a loss of esteem. Maybe we will sit down by the roadside and wonder why we make no progress. Perhaps we will look for another path that seems less burdensome or make a nice one for ourselves. Saint Benedict is not encroaching on our freedom. He is simply giving us directions about how to get to the place where we want to arrive. Everything depends on the conditions he enunciated earlier in the Prologue: "*If* you desire true and perpetual life" (RB Prol. 17) and *if* you "desire to see good days" (RB Prol. 15), then this is the way to realize your dream. If such is not your ambition and you prefer to take another path, then go ahead. "You are free, go your own way" (RB 58.10), as Saint Benedict will later say to a prospective candidate.

If, however, this path is the way for you, then why not run along it with confidence and joy? Admittedly this is easier later in the journey than earlier. Saint Benedict will discuss its initial restrictiveness in a few verses. The reality is, however, that if we have truly discovered our vocation, if this way is

God's plan for us, then we should be immensely grateful that we are not condemned to puddling around in the darkness looking for the path, using up our limited energy, and getting nowhere. Happy are they who quickly discover the way to go and stay on it; their progress will be unimpeded. As Saint Anselm says in one of his letters, "Let them be happy to have found somewhere to live throughout their whole life, not unwillingly but willingly, without anxiety about needing to move from one place to another" (*Ep.* 37).

We have often noted how, in the Prologue, Saint Benedict is trying to motivate us to follow the path he is indicating in a spirit of enthusiasm and with generosity of heart. This is not simply because monastic life is always delightful—we know it is not—but because it is a sure means at finding a place in the heavenly kingdom. This is to say that monastic life makes sense only in an eschatological context. In pondering the special quality of monastic life, Saint Bernard of Clairvaux (in *Apologia* 1) reminds us of the important text of 1 Corinthians 15:19: "If for this life only we have hope in Christ Jesus, then of all people are we the most to be pitied." If there is no future life, there is no point worrying about the quality of our present behavior. We can make our own the chant Saint Paul quotes a few verses later: "Let us eat and drink for tomorrow we die" (1 Cor 15:32 = Isa 22:13).

Monastic life makes no sense except in the context of eternity. This also applies to Christian life in general. Without belief in a future life and confidence in the road that leads to it, there is no point in walking the way of Christian discipleship. You might remember the title of chapter 7 of the Second Vatican Council's Constitution on the Church, *Lumen Gentium*: "The Eschatological Character of the Pilgrim Church and its Union with the Heavenly Church." The church also makes no sense unless it is the vehicle that transports us to heaven. The most important information about a bus is the sign in front that tells us where it is going. The bus's color and the relative comfort of its seats are irrelevant unless the bus will take us where we want to go. So it is with the church. The Pilgrim Church is a body in movement; it is on a journey. And where is it going? It is on the road to heaven. It is from its destination that it gets its specificity and identity. In the desiring mind of believers, we are not only on a journey to heaven; in the strength of our anticipation we are already there. As Saint Paul says, "Our citizenship is in heaven" (Phil 3:20).

Monastic life is a journey to heaven; its inconveniences are more than compensated for by the hope we have of what awaits us at journey's end. It is in the strength of that hope that we quicken our pace. To run with zeal along the road that leads to eternal life requires, first of all, a strong faith in the reality of eternal life; we need to believe that this life here on earth, so concrete and so precious, is but the first phase of our existence. We believe that this life will come to an end and that after death will come judgment, then resurrection from the dead, and, after that, life everlasting. It is this belief that sustained the martyrs in their toils and travails; it is this buoyant hope that energizes the monk in his lifelong commitment to the monastic way.

45

Therefore a school of the Lord's service is to be set up by us.

This is a verse that has occasioned quite a bit of comment, partly because its meaning seems so clear; yet perhaps there is more to this verse than immediately meets the eye.

First, the phrase *constituenda est* is rather formal; it is the sort of construction to be found in legal preambles: having considered all the facts, there is a need to make certain provisions, in this case, to set up a "school of the Lord's service." It is as though Saint Benedict is saying that because of the scope of the spiritual journey and the challenges to be confronted in making that journey, some sort of formal institution needs to be established in which the wayfarer can be provided with the optimal conditions for reaching the desired destination. It is almost as though he is saying that progress to eternal life depends on the acceptance of certain necessary structures that have the effect of channeling the choices made, in a way that prevents time and energy being lost in aimless meandering.

This is a way of looking at the spiritual life that does not appeal to everyone—particularly those who deem themselves to be "free spirits." In fact, these people are usually far from free, being often subject to the vagaries of their own unexamined impulses. For Saint Benedict the only means of progress in the monastic or spiritual path was through the acceptance of discipline; undisciplined initiatives usually end up self-cancelling. The Latin word *disciplina* is built upon the underlying verb *discere*, which means "to learn." The acceptance of being under discipline is a sign of a willingness to enter into a process of learning. This means consenting to be instructed, guided, taught. One who follows the way of Saint Benedict is one who is prepared to be a disciple, a learner in the school of Christ. In fact, thirteen times in the Rule, the monk is referred to simply as a disciple (RB 2.5, 6, 11, 12, 13; 3.6; 5.9, 16, 17; 6.3, 6, 8; 36:10).

Here we must try to understand the special nuance that the Latin word *schola* had for Saint Benedict so many centuries ago. This is the only time he employs the word. It was not primarily a term that was used for one of a network of institutions entrusted by society with the basic and obligatory education of children. It had not, by then, lost the connotation that came to it from its Greek root *schole*, and that was the notion of leisure. A "school" was a place where it was possible to have the opportunity to learn from a teacher, to engage in intelligent conversation and in the "liberal" arts, to be free to attend to matters more important than urgent. The sense is that this is a space in which one can attend to the things that really matter. A *schola* is not so much an institution that injects a predetermined curriculum into the minds of its students as a place where they can grow by learning, where their inherent potential is educed by education. It is impossible to miss the humane content of this term. Although the training methods may seem restrictive, the goal is the fullest possible realization of those who attend.

Where there is a school, there must be a master or instructor. Who in the monastery is the teacher? First and foremost, Christ is the monk's teacher and so the fundamental exercise of monastic life is to continue steadfastly on the spiritual journey under "the guidance of the Gospel" (RB Prol. 21). He is never to move away from this masterful teaching (RB Prol. 50) but to remain a lifelong disciple in the school of Christ: always willing to hear, always attentive, always ready to obey, always open to change.

The abbot, as the one whose duty it is to perform the functions of Christ in the monastery, is also a teacher: "He should be learned in the divine law so that he may bring forth new things and old" (RB 64.9). In the Middle Ages the manner of the abbot's teaching was specified; he taught the monks in chapter, both by daily comments on the part of the Rule read that day and by more developed discourses on the major feasts. Curiously, Saint Benedict does not give any details about how the abbot's teaching office was to be fulfilled, whether by conferences given to the community or by personal instruction in the manner of the Desert Fathers. Since the abbot was not usually a priest, he was not the one who preached sermons or homilies in a liturgical context.

Notwithstanding this lack of detail, the Rule is quite clear on the importance of this ongoing function. This is what Saint

Benedict says in chapter 2, "What Kind of Person an Abbot Should Be":

> Therefore, when someone receives the name of abbot, he should be superior to his disciples by a twofold teaching: that is, he should show forth [his teaching] by all good and holy deeds more than by words. For capable disciples let him propound the Lord's commandments by words, but for the hardhearted and the more simple let him demonstrate the divine precepts by his deeds. . . . In his teaching the abbot should always maintain the apostolic form, which says "Argue, appeal, rebuke." That is, he should adapt to the moment, both coaxing and arousing terror, mixing the sternness of a master with the kindliness of a father. (RB 2.11-12, 23-24)

The content of the abbot's teaching is the divine law as contained in the Scriptures. Saint Benedict is quite emphatic about this. "The abbot should not teach or establish as policy or command anything outside the Lord's precept" (RB 2.4). So, the Benedictine abbot is not some sort of guru molding disciples according to his own particular gifts and orientation. He is a channel by which Gospel teaching, as transmitted by the monastic forebears (RB 73.2), is translated and applied to the lives of those under his care. No one individual is indispensable. We are all learners; Christ is the permanent teacher and master of all. When one abbot goes, another takes his place, but monastic doctrine—if it is according to the mind of Saint Benedict—remains constant.

The abbot is not the only teacher in the monastery. All those who are selected for the key offices in the community are to be chosen on the basis of their sound practice and their skill in teaching. It is not always enough to do the right thing; sometimes it is necessary also to be able to explain verbally the beliefs and values that underlie a particular course of action. And it happens that sometimes we learn by teaching.

It is by expounding values to others that we come to an understanding of their relevance in our own lives (RB 2.40).

The monastery is the school where we are trained in the service of Christ: to take our part in the Work of God, to serve one another in humility, to embrace wholeheartedly the elements of the monastic lifestyle, and to learn to live in love. It is a school from which we never graduate. We are always learning something new. And it is through such life-long learning that we grow in grace in the sight of God and of those around us.

46

In its organization we hope to put in place noth-ing that is harsh or heavy.

This verse begins a very precious part of the Prologue, one that is original to Saint Benedict, added to his source-text, the Rule of the Master. These verses, together with the ending he added to the chapter on humility, give one of the clearest in-dications of Saint Benedict's perspective on the dynamics of the monastic or spiritual life. It is a progression from external discipline to inner conviction and from there to a very profound sense of delight in God and in spiritual reality. Most of the Rule paints a rather stern picture of its author as one who lays down the law and expects it to be observed. Here we see something different. External regulations are necessary in order to lay solid foundations and get people started on the right track. When the beliefs and values have been internalized and a certain facility with the practices of the spiritual life develops, it becomes pos-sible to be more relaxed about regularity and routines and to begin to enjoy the fruits of so many years of effort.

In his chapters on the amount of food and drink and in other places, Saint Benedict professes himself reluctant to lay down detailed regulations since he recognizes that people have different needs and receive different gifts of grace. In this present verse the same diffidence appears. He does not want to make the transition into a new life form unnecessarily difficult, perhaps because he recognizes that every person's life will have its own particular challenges and that it is in dealing with these that character is built. Artificial or external trials do not have the same character-building effect; they are little more than elaborate games.

When somebody begins deliberately to live a more fervent spiritual life, whether or not this change of pace involves entering a monastery, there is a period of initial enthusiasm that helps the person to adjust to the changes involved. This is normal and to be expected, but it is also temporary. The real work of self-knowledge and purification is yet to begin.

The fundamental challenge of monastic life or spiritual life in general derives from the emergence into the open of hidden negativities. For this to happen, a certain exterior blandness is necessary. An unexciting exterior life, when a person is relaxed and not distracted by multiple concerns and activities, is the optimal condition for the appearance of tendencies that have no opportunity to show themselves when too much else is going on. This revelation of their shadow comes as a surprise to most people because, in the past, they lived in a state of ignorance of self or denial. The more or less dramatic advent of contrary imaginations and temptations is shocking. What is happening? Just when they begin to take their spiritual life more seriously at a practical level, it begins to disintegrate before their eyes. What is happening is that the real action is just beginning. Experience reveals that to help people pass through this phase creatively, firm but moderate structures are needed, plus unconditional but sober support and affirmation. The crisis is normal, but its specific features are proper to each person. Meanwhile, nothing should be done to terminate the phase before its work is complete.

This is what Saint Benedict offers in his Rule—a lifestyle based on the Gospel and on solid monastic experience, expressed through structures and institutions that are all stamped with his signature quality of moderation. Saint Gregory the Great noted that the Rule's chief character is its discretion: it asks of its adherents neither too much nor too little.

It is important to view this moderation in the right light. To be moderate is not the same as to be wishy-washy: vague about values, ignorant about how to translate these into practice, and naive about the inherent precariousness of human virtue. It is not some sort of mindless benevolence that is unable to distinguish what is right from what is wrong and what works from what does not. The moderation that is typical of Saint Benedict and all genuine spiritual masters is the result of recognizing the complexity of moral life. The simple fact is that any virtue that is carried to extreme becomes a vice. Too much abstemiousness quickly becomes avarice. Too much diligence easily slips into rigidity or even scrupulosity. Likewise, wherever there is a virtue drawing the person in one direction, there is probably a different virtue pulling in the opposite direction. An act of spontaneous generosity may need to be checked by prudence, faithful observance of a precept may need to be tempered by compassion toward one's neighbor, and hard work may need to be balanced by leisure.

When we say that moderation is the hallmark of Saint Benedict's Rule—especially when we compare it with the Rule of the Master—we are saying that it is a text that reflects a great deal of experience as well as a sure knowledge of human nature. Saint Benedict knows that the best recipe for perseverance in the spiritual journey is to have a moderate measure of *all* the virtues rather than lots of one virtue and none of another. What good is zeal without discretion or knowledge without compassion? In addition, it is probably true of most people that they pass through different seasons in their life in which different virtues are called for. It is a little like what happens during sleep. We do not lie motionless during the hours of sleep, but we move about, now stretching one set of muscles and then resting them. In the same way, we do not develop virtues by systematically following some sort of flow chart. What happens is that different situations call forth different responses and so different virtues are cultivated. Quiet times ask for discipline and regularity, sickness calls for patience, irritation for calm, conflict for humility and tolerance. Perceived injustice is an occasion for me to practice evangelical forgiveness. And so we go through life learning to be stretched by the situations in which we find ourselves. We never become spectacularly proficient in any virtue, but gradually, by using all the various tools of good work, we are changed and grace more often has its way with us.

Saint Benedict, the patron saint of moderation, wishes to prescribe nothing harsh or heavy because he knows that it is by small increments of fidelity in the everyday virtues that we make most progress along the road that leads to eternal life.

It may be a little restrictive—as reason and equity dictate—for the purpose of advancing the process of amending vices and for maintaining charity.

Anybody who has ever entered a monastery or has begun to implement a resolution to live a more spiritual life soon realizes that changes have to be made in everyday conduct.

The determination to live a better life means that many previously gratifying courses of action have to be reduced or eliminated. This is not necessarily because they are sinful or self-destructive, but it is simply because to do the things we have determined to do we need time. It is not easy to find time, so we have to make time instead. This means changing the practical priorities of our day in order to give scope to what has become most important for us.

This involves regularity. Anything that is not immediately gratifying is an easy prey for procrastination. The one way to persevere in a course of action with only long-term results is to build it into a routine so that there is little deliberation involved in getting started. This is as true in the spiritual life as in every other activity. Abbot John Chapman of Downside famously wrote in the 1930s, "The only way to pray is to pray; and the way to pray well is to pray much. If one has no time for this, then one must at least pray regularly. But the less one prays the worse it goes" (*Letter* 12, p. 53).

Regularity means living by a *regula*, a rule. It means having a structure to support our program of spiritual exercises so that they are not dependent on the whim of the moment or liable to be displaced by something more urgent but less important. Adopting such a manner of life is, as Saint Benedict observes, necessarily restrictive, not because placing limitations on our freedom is a good thing in itself, but because it serves the purpose of checking the growth of vice and preserving charity and harmony in the community.

Vice is somewhat natural to us and its hold over us increases when habits are formed. When undesirable actions become habitual, they bypass many of the processes that might prevent their happening. The only way to break a habit is to slow everything down and to take steps to eliminate those factors that nourish the habit. This involves a curtailment of our freedom. Since the monastery is in the business of amending vices, it must necessarily be a place where some restriction of personal freedom is anticipated and accepted. A monastery that allowed us to do what we liked if and when we liked would become a laughingstock and would fail to fulfill its purpose for existence. A spiritual life that consisted merely in pious whitewashing of an otherwise sinful existence is, as Jesus noted, nothing more than an exercise in hypocrisy. If we are to reduce the hold of negative tendencies over us, we have to welcome a measure of self-control and discipline.

Constraint is also a necessary consequence of social living. When we consent to be part of a group, to some extent, we submerge our personal preferences in those of the group. Self-will must give way to the common will. To run with the herd requires us to accept group norms and submit to accepted lines of authority. On a higher plane, to find love in a community we have to be or become aware of the feelings and needs of other persons and to subordinate our own needs and feelings to make life more pleasant for them. Such restrictiveness is not a narrowing; it is, rather, a broadening of our affective range away from ourselves toward other people.

If we are to live relatively free from the tyranny of vice and in an ambience of peace and harmony with others, Saint Benedict avers that we need to accept some limitations on our personal freedom. There is a paradox here. To be truly free we must give up our freedom. To be free *from* sin and free *for* others we cannot follow every unexamined inclination that presents itself to our awareness. This is a theme that is expressed several times in the New Testament: "See that the exercise of your freedom does not become a stumbling block to the weak" (1 Cor 8:9). "You, my brothers and sisters, were called to be free. But do not use your freedom to indulge the flesh; rather, serve one another in love" (Gal 5:13). "Behave as free people, but do not use your freedom as a cover-up for evil; live as servants of God" (1 Pet 2:16).

Freedom's limits are those imposed by reason and equity. This is an important principle. Free choice is God's gift to us;

it is an integral part of human existence. We may not ground-lessly renounce that freedom or seek to take away the freedom of another. There are, however, occasions in which it is reason-able to make a free choice to restrict its exercise. These will be determined, as Saint Benedict notes, by reason and equity.

Saint Benedict thinks that the kind of community that best sustains us in our spiritual search is one that is charac-terized by the twin qualities of reasonableness and fairness. Throughout the Rule he shows himself willing to deviate from an abstract ideal if, in the concrete situation, there are reasonable grounds for doing so. Everything is to be done "with measure and reason" (RB 70.5). Even what had been considered unexpected or undesirable is acceptable, if it is reasonable (RB 61.4; 65.14). Likewise, he is alert to the paramount importance of visible fairness in the community regimen. This is achieved by transparency in governance, the avoidance of favoritism (RB 2.20; 34.2), and a willingness to give honor and respect to all, irrespective of their position in the community (RB 4.8; 72.4). Fairness is not an enforced egalitarianism that imposes a uniform observance on all with-out exception but rather a sensitivity to different capacities and gifts that allows all to contribute to the community's life to the fullest extent of their capacity.

Virtues are habits; habits are formed by repeated actions. It may well be that once a virtue is established the perfor-mance of actions is easy and even delightful. It is quite dif-ferent before the virtue has taken root. In the earlier stages there is a need to struggle against inertia and against contrary tendencies. The performance of virtuous acts is hard work; it goes against our inclinations, and we have to insist on volun-tary restrictions on our freedom in order to break the tyranny of previous habits. This means being firm in following the regimen we have reasonably adopted and being patient while new neural pathways are being formed in our brains that will slowly render good actions easier.

Restrictions that are reasonable and fair are not harsh and heavy. They are the necessary conditions of continuing growth in human maturity and in spiritual life. Perhaps it is time for us to stop rebelling against everything that seems to limit spontaneity. A regular life has the effect of channeling our energies. The result is that life becomes more intensely personal, it goes further and faster, and fewer of our personal resources are dissipated through lack of purpose.

48

Do not run away from this road to salvation, fearful and terrified. At the very beginning it cannot be other than narrow.

The challenges faced by one who chooses to walk the spiritual path are not inconsiderable—not today, nor were they ever. Those of us who once so wholeheartedly embraced the road that leads to salvation are always in danger of losing our enthusiasm. As a result, we find ourselves disenchanted and disconsolate because of the difficulties we face.

Our first instinct is to regard the hardship as, in some way, abnormal. It should not be there. Life should be easier and more pleasant than this! Following on the heels of this thought is the suggestion that someone else is to blame for this sorry situation. We take for granted that we ourselves are beyond reproach. Therefore the problem lies with another person, or the community, or the way of life that we have adopted. The solution to the problem is to abandon our spiritual project, at least in its present form, reckon our lost efforts as experience, and move on. It all seems so reasonable. We thought we saw the way ahead; we tried it and it led nowhere, so we reverse course and either find another path or move our life in a completely different direction.

Saint Benedict's response to this conclusion is to speak personally to each one; the verb is in the second-person singular. He says, "Don't run away." He does not mislead the person in crisis by saying, "Don't worry. The problem is nothing; it will soon go away." This would be to create a false hope and to immure the person more fully in delusion. He simply says, "Stay." The fact is that in most problem situations it is we ourselves who are the key components. When we run away from one set of difficulties we may find a little temporary relief, but, mysteriously, the same issues eventually arise again in the new situation. We can never run away from ourselves and so, wherever we go, we take our liabilities with us.

When we begin to make real progress on the monastic or spiritual path we can expect that we will be confronted with some of the negativity that has hitherto been hidden from us. As our spiritual sight becomes sharper, we see more fully the extent to which we need to be transformed if we are to come to the full realization of our potential. It is as though, after a long period of blind wayfaring through mist and fog, we come to a place where we can see clearly, only to discover how far away our destination is and how much more travail is ahead of us. Saint Benedict says, "Do not run away fearful and terrified," but stay where you are, suffer the indignity of present imperfection, and allow grace to work its wonders in its own good time.

Many people give up the spiritual pursuit simply because they lose their nerve. The fact is that the path which leads to eternal life is not straightforward. More often than not what contributes to progress is counterintuitive and risky. We do not advance at the same pace and sometimes we have to lose ground to go forward. The further we travel along this path the more necessary it is that we have a competent spiritual guide; if we cannot find one in the flesh, we may have to be content with learning from books the wisdom of ancient spiritual masters. Whatever possibilities our situation offers, we would be very foolish to think that we have nothing to learn, that we can work things out for ourselves, that we simply draw up a blueprint for our life and then follow it. This is especially true when—for no apparent reason—everything seems to go wrong. Fortunate are we if, at such a juncture, there is someone to indicate to us the life-giving potential of our situation and to say personally to us, with Saint Benedict, "Stay where you are. Do not run away fearful and terrified."

We soon learn that to keep us from becoming slack God makes sure that challenges always catch us wrong-footed. On our good days we are able to cope with all kinds of troubles without even breaking into a sweat. So, in fair weather they leave us undisturbed. When temptations do come, they always arrive at just the wrong moment, when we are not ready to handle them. At such a time we are easily overpowered and quickly become discouraged afterward.

We have to be prepared to pass through initial hardship in order to arrive at a point where we experience a higher degree of facility in living as we ought. Saint Gregory the Great has an interesting take on why the initial phases of spiritual life and any later step toward holier living are so difficult. He contrasts ordinary desire with spiritual desire. Ordinary desire, he says, is warm and attractive from the start and easily bears us along with it. When it attains its object it quickly grows cold and we lose interest. As the old song has it, "After you get what you want, you don't want it!" Spiritual desire is the opposite. We become conscious of the desire yet find ourselves sluggish when it comes to taking the practical steps to bring about the desired result. It is easier to be enthusiastic about prayer than to actually pray. When the moment comes for us to translate our desire into practice, there are a thousand counterattractions that attempt to pull us in other directions. Many people are attracted by the prospect of a religious vocation, which seems to pull together all the disparate strands of their life, yet they never take the next step and are therefore left wondering and a little dissatisfied for the rest of their lives. With ordinary desires we are carried by the momentum of the desire; with spiritual desire we are paralyzed by inertia. A lot of effort is required to get ourselves moving.

Since most of us are allergic to more than an occasional burst of effort, we find this very discouraging. And we share with many of our contemporaries a reluctance to continue with something that seems not to be immediately gratifying. We give up. This is where Saint Benedict's message about stability is vitally important. Beset as we are with the typically modern fear of making a commitment that goes beyond the present moment, we are more likely to run away from a serious challenge than to grapple with it. Of course, we do not think of it as running away; we prefer to say that we are exploring alternative options. The effect is the same. We do not stay at anything long enough for it to begin to work its magic on us.

Interestingly, the first thing that Saint Benedict asks of a prospective candidate is that he makes a promise to persevere (RB 58.9). This is not yet a vow; that comes later. It is a commitment to stay with the process until it becomes clear whether the monastic way is the one that the candidate really wants to follow. If the candidate finally chooses to withdraw, this needs to be a mature decision (RB 58.14), not a hasty retreat on the basis of contrary first impressions.

It is normal for beginnings to be narrow. Every new beginning as we go through life asks us to accept some restrictions on the freedom we previously enjoyed in order to focus our attention and concentrate our energies on the way forward. The road that leads to salvation and eternal life is no different. Every time the Holy Spirit brings about a surge in our interior energies we will be required to narrow our options for the time being. The benefits of this channeling of energies will become apparent only with time.

As progress is made in the way of life and in faith, the road of God's commandments will be run with heart enlarged and in the indescribable sweetness of love.

Spiritual life is not static. There is development at the level of experience. Externally life continues much as it has done for many years, but interiorly there is a new capacity to find delight in what previously seemed hard and laborious. This is a theme to which Saint Benedict will return at the end of his chapter on humility:

> Now, therefore, after ascending all these steps of humility, the monk will quickly arrive at that perfect love of God which casts out fear. Through this love, all that he used to observe somewhat fearfully he will now begin to fulfill without effort, as though naturally, from habit. [He will act] no longer out of fear of hell, but out of love for Christ, from good habit itself and delight in virtue. (RB 7.67-68)

This happy outcome is not dramatic or boisterous but a profound and serene contentment that is fueled by the increasing frequency of moments in which God seems very close. This is the reason for the fervor to be seen among the seniors of a monastery, which far excels the initial spurt of enthusiasm experienced by newcomers. They have grown into the way of life, and its observance is no longer a struggle but is experienced as a privilege and a source of happiness.

Spiritual life is not static. Development occurs. Saint Benedict draws our attention to five particular areas of spiritual growth.

First, we make progress in living out the everyday imperatives that follow from our commitment to Christian discipleship. This means that our seeking of God is less a sporadic event in an otherwise distracted life, but it becomes the ordering principle in the choice of our lifestyle. I do this because it helps me to live in mindfulness; I avoid that because it consumes my energies and diffuses the focus of my mind and heart. The term used by Saint Benedict is *conversatio,* by which he means the integrity of monastic life, the sum of its observances, everything that gives expression to the specificity of the monk's vocation. We could say, in a more general sense, that it is the lifestyle adopted by one who is taking seriously the call of the Gospel. As the years pass and grace reshapes our lives, there is a higher consistency between what we believe and hold dear and the way we live. And what a wonder that is!

Second, there is an increase in faith. In a minimalist sense we could take this word as meaning our fidelity, so that what the text is referring to is our increasing faithfulness to the commitments we have made. It is much better to understand the term simply as faith—the deep interior conviction that follows from God's dwelling within us. Faith is not so much a state of intellect so that we know something without tangible evidence. It is more an act of will by which we give assent to something on the basis of subjective certainty rather than objective proof. I was always sure that my mother loved me, although I could scarcely have proved it by logical argument. In the same way, my faith is the result of having experienced the reality of the God of love and having given assent to this reality. My faith grows the more I have that experience; it grows through withdrawal from sensate involvement and opening my awareness to the spiritual world. Faith grows strong through prayer. If the *conversatio* I follow leads me to deeper and more frequent prayer then I will grow in faith. I will slowly become more aware of the presence of the loving God. This, in turn, will energize me to embrace with greater zest the means that enable me to make the most of God's wonderful gift.

And so we come to the third element: love. The more we experience love the more loving we become—not just in returning love to those who love us, but universally. When somebody fell in love in the old-fashioned musicals, this was signaled by singing and dancing in the street, embracing strangers, and looking with a kindly eye upon life in general. For the person in love it seems that the sun always shines. At least that is what we were told. In a certain sense it is true. One who lives in the presence of the God of love fears nothing, is immune to destructive self-doubt, and is better able to cope with unprovoked misunderstanding and hostility. The reason the commandments of love are indivisible is that, strictly speaking, it is impossible to love and hate simultaneously. The kind of love that can coexist with hatred is not genuine love: it is self-serving and selective; it excludes as well as includes. This is why Jesus' precept of love tells us to embrace our enemies and persecutors so as to transform them into friends and collaborators. To the extent that I am estranged from another, I am estranged from myself because "no man is an island." When I cannot forgive someone who has harmed me and maybe is still harming me, I am allowing bitterness entrance into my heart, and, if I do not change, it will eventually consume me. On the other hand, when love finds entrance into the inmost recesses of my being, I admit into my life a source of change and integration. And then, even in the midst of contradiction and turmoil, I find a deeper serenity that enables me to believe that "all will be well."

When the heart is enlarged by love it begins to experience the fourth effect of progress in God's grace: indescribable sweetness and delight. The closer we are to eternal life the more we are filled with gladness. This does not exclude external trials or persecutions, illness or diminishment, but beneath these heavy burdens there is an incredible lightness that makes us cry out, "In all these we have been victorious because of God who has loved us" (RB 7.39). The delight is indescribable because, from an ordinary perspective it makes no sense. This is because such joy comes from very deep within, one of the fruits of the Holy Spirit's action, not ascribable to any visible source of happiness. God is joy and those who abide in God abide in joy and God abides in them.

And so they run. We have spoken of Saint Benedict's use of this verb previously. It points to the fifth effect of spiritual development: energy. Instead of growing weary with the length of the road and the sameness of its landscape, we find our pace quickening as we come closer to our destination; the midlife demon of acedia has been left behind. As Saint Paul says, "While our outward humanity wastes away, our interior humanity is being renewed day after day" (2 Cor 4:16). We find the same sentiment in the second part of Isaiah: "Though youths grow faint and are weary, and the young drop exhausted, those who hope in the Lord will renew their strength; they will fly on eagles' wings" (Isa 40:30-31).

"Nothing is hard to those who love," says Saint Jerome (*Ep.* 22.40). And Saint Augustine concurs, "There is no labor for one who loves" (*In Jn* 48.1). This is the message that Saint Benedict wants to convey: at the beginning of the journey the road may be narrow, and, in the many years that follow, it may well be experienced as hard and rough, but, in the end, the road itself becomes a source of joy and fulfillment. As the psalmist says, "I will run on the road of your commandments because you have enlarged my heart" (Ps 118:32).

50

And so, let us never cease to have [Christ] as master, let us persevere in his doctrine in the monastery until death, and let us participate by patience in the sufferings of Christ. In this way will we deserve to be sharers in his kingdom. Amen.

Taking one's place in the kingdom of God is, according to John Cassian, the ultimate goal of monastic life, as it is of all Christian life. The question is this: how do we arrive at this destination? Throughout the Prologue, Saint Benedict has been attempting to give a general answer to this question so as to provide a framework for the practical prescriptions that will follow. His two great recommendations are mindfulness and energy. We need to be awake and aware of the possibilities that each hour and each day bring. And, aware of the challenges by a good level of self-knowledge, we need to exert ourselves to be active in doing good and avoiding evil.

In this final verse of the Prologue he takes a step back to situate our labors and struggles in a Christocentric context. Ultimately, attaining the goal of eternal life is not a triumph of personal achievement; it comes from the closeness of our relationship with Christ. Entering his kingdom presupposes that we are conformed to him, that our life has become progressively more Christlike. In other words, Saint Benedict is here emphasizing a theme that has been mentioned several times in the Prologue. There is continuity between the way we live now and the state that will be ours for all eternity.

Becoming Christlike is not a matter of calling vast crowds to conversion or performing splendid deeds of compassionate power. It is primarily a willingness to enter into a fuller participation of the paschal paradox, into which we were initiated at baptism. Saint Benedict's Prologue does not emphasize the linkage between baptism and the monastic life as much as the Rule of the Master, but it clearly formed an implicit background to his thinking. As Christians, we are called to see our lives in terms of the dying and rising of Christ: we die to self and to the "world" in order to live for God. The two phases are inseparable. We cannot enter with the risen Christ into the fullness of God without first emptying ourselves, with Christ, of all that is not God.

Thus our Christian life, our monastic life, is stamped with the image of the cross of Christ. This does not mean that the Christian and the monk necessarily have to suffer more than other human beings. It means that the suffering inevitable to every human life is viewed in a different light. Instead of being resented and rejected, it is welcomed (in a certain sense) as a means of being united with the suffering Christ. To express it differently: we can render our suffering meaningful by associating our pain with that of Christ, seeing it as therapeutic and redemptive rather than as purely destructive. Negativity is more easily borne when we can say with Saint Paul, "In my flesh I fill up what is lacking to the afflictions of Christ for the sake of his body, the Church" (Col 1:24).

It is through the practice of patience that we draw close to Christ. Saint Benedict, curiously enough, sees the monastery as, above all, a place that calls us to the practice of this virtue. In the fourth step of humility, he lists all the petty occasions in community life that make patience imperative—otherwise we will soon become rebellious, cynical, and bitter. Patience is not a trivial virtue for Saint Benedict; in a sense, it is the culmination and consummation of all the virtues. The practice of the cardinal virtues from which all other moral virtues spring—justice, fortitude, prudence, and temperance—is dependent on our willingness to transcend the pleasure principle and endure hard times in order to bring about what is good and true. If we cannot say no to our hedonistic impulses or our vindictive tendencies and so endure deprivation and harsh treatment, it is unlikely that we will make any progress at all toward a more Christlike existence.

Patience means that we break the causal chain of evil. When something bad is done to us, we are likely to want to do something bad to someone else. If we have to suffer then, perversely, our suffering becomes more tolerable if we make others suffer as well. If I am in a bad mood, it is somewhat alleviated by making everyone around me miserable. And so suffering is passed from one to another, from one generation to the next. The beauty of patience is that it calls a halt to this nonsense. It absorbs pain instead of passing it on. I am hurt, insulted, humiliated. Instead of striking at someone else—or even kicking the cat—I simply embrace patience with a quiet mind. The pain goes no further. This particular chain of suffering terminates with me. Instead of being vindictive I ensure that whatever I endure remains within me. When struck on one cheek, I offer the other. To one who steals my tunic, I give my cloak. When forced to go one mile, I go two (7.42). I am not using my setbacks in order to become a professional victim and so able to claim entitlements on that account. I am simply refusing to assert my rights for the sake of peace and in the hope that my lack of resistance will lower the level of violence. I choose to absorb evil rather than pass it on and so perpetuate it. Saint Benedict understood that this path of nonviolence was the way on which Christ walked and on which he calls his disciples to follow.

Many people are surprised and even disappointed that the way mapped out by Saint Benedict is not more mystical. There are no tricks on the way to contemplative prayer; it is simply a matter of learning from the One who is meek and humble of heart not to pay back evil with evil, nor harsh words with reproaches or withdrawal. It means accepting whatever hardship comes our way as a means of conforming ourselves more fully to Christ, of being Christlike in our response to others even though they are not Christlike in their attitude to us. Choosing this path reshapes our wills to bring them into conformity with the will of Christ. This is the foundation of all contemplative experience.

For most of us this means a radical change in attitude that begins at the start of our spiritual journey and continues until the end. Instead of being slaves to self-will or puppets of social conditioning, we take Christ as our master and remain his disciples throughout life. We do this, of course, through our fidelity in exposing ourselves to Christ's teaching. "Each hour and at every moment we open up the soil of our hearts with the plough of the Gospel," as John Cassian says, "that is, with the constant remembering of the Lord's passion" (*Conference* 1.22).

Progress along the spiritual path is a matter of personal fidelity to Christ, daily listening to his teaching in the gospels, reshaping our lives in accordance with that teaching so that we become more like Christ in our self-forgetfulness, our generosity of spirit, and our meekness of disposition. For Saint Benedict this was accomplished by following his "little rule for beginners," persevering in it despite apparent setbacks, and never losing hope in the mercy of God. Thus, by sharing in the passion of Christ, we prepare ourselves to be part of his kingdom. And may the Lord lead us all together to eternal life. Amen.